"Most of the projects that fail, in ɪ managers have underestimated the complexity oɪ ɪne pɪoɟɛɛɪ anu overestimated the capability of their organisation to cope with the changes. What was needed was a simple way to assess these in terms the Board would understand – and Peter has delivered it. Highly recommended!"

Roy Ayliffe,
former Director of Professional Practice,
The Chartered Institute of Purchasing & Supply (CIPS)

"On the rollercoaster of change projects, too often the success or failure of initiatives is left to chance for the lack of methods or tools to evaluate progress and re-calibrate as necessary. Peter's book provides these tools, along with a comprehensive and pragmatic 360-degree view of the change process that offers many options to do something about risky projects before they fail, before or during the process. Every manager with a tough project should read this before they start, and for anyone with a project already going pear-shaped this book offers a real chance to do something practical about it."

David Hain,
Director, Transformation Partners

"This book helps, informs and educates managers with concepts, tools and methodology that would have saved them valuable time and effort in their projects. *The Change Equation* offers real-world insights on how to turn complex management Projects from theory into practical business solutions. A worthy read for all managers."

Nym Lotay
BT Major Programme and Projects Manager,
and NHS-PCT Non Executive Director.

"I like the way that Peter has brought together proven methods into an integrated approach to Organization Change. With this book Organization Change Management has come of age."

Nikki Cole,
Director, BlueSky Cat Limited

"Peter has developed a neat idea – a way to assess a project's complexity and relate it to an organisation's capability. This book provides a simple, sanguine read for anyone responsible for managing change. It offers good theory for the consultant, and good tips for the intelligent practitioner, but its real value is in the insights for senior management who want to ensure their transformation programme will succeed."

Graham Colclough,
Vice President, Global Public Sector, Capgemini UK plc

THE CHANGE EQUATION

A practical and innovative approach
to quantifying and overcoming
cultural and capability barriers
to organisational change

Peter Duschinsky

First published in 2009 by Management Books 2000 Ltd
Forge House, Limes Road
Kemble, Cirencester
Gloucestershire, GL7 6AD, UK
Tel: 0044 (0) 1285 771441
Fax: 0044 (0) 1285 771055
Email: info@mb2000.com
Web: www.mb2000.com

British Library Cataloguing in Publication Data is available

ISBN 9781852526245

About the book

In these times of economic upheaval, change is inevitable. It's being forced on all of us. The last thing we need is for change projects to fail. But research by leading commentators on management suggests that 90% of change programmes face major implementation problems and only 30% of such projects produce a positive bottom-line improvement.

In this easy-to-read, practical book, Peter Duschinsky provides a route-map for senior managers to de-risk their IT-based change projects and improve the returns on their investment in modernisation and performance improvement.

Peter brings together models and tools – some well-known, others you will encounter for the first time – to help you understand and measure the capability of your organisation to handle change. You will find out how to assess the complexity and risks of your projects and what you need to do differently to ensure success.

If you are responsible for leading your organisation out of the recession, this book may help you get there. Can you afford not to read it?

About the author

Peter Duschinsky is a management consultant with two careers under his belt and many years of experience of bringing best practice and new ways of working into business and the public sector. In 2003, Peter set up The Imaginist Company in order to focus on helping smaller companies survive and thrive in e-business. His work helped to influence government policy towards smaller suppliers. Frustrated by the apparent inability of local councils and other complex organisations to modernise and improve, Peter set out to find out what the real barriers to change were and to understand what could be done to change this sad state of affairs. Three years and a lot of research and experimentation later, this book is the result.

Peter lives in London with his wife, Val, whose encouragement and support made this book possible. They are extraordinarily proud of their two offspring, who are off changing the world – one as a global philanthropy consultant and the other as a Director of Psychology at a London clinic, working with stress-related illness. By comparison, helping managers to get their projects to succeed is child's play!

Contents

9

1

Introduction

This book shows you how to take two models which describe an organisation's capability – the organisational culture evolution spiral and the business process capability ladder – and combine them to provide a baseline from which you can assess the complexity and risks of a transformation project – the Change Equation. The ability to analyse and quantify the gap between capability and project complexity is the 'big idea' of the book. It's simple – when you know how.

When I sat down to write this book I was driven by a sense of deep frustration. The companies and public sector organisations that I had encountered, both as a consultant and as a customer, talked a lot about the changes they were planning in order to improve their performance and transform customer service, but they didn't actually seem to be achieving very much. As I ploughed through the research on project failure and collected sometimes spectacular examples and depressing stories of budgets overspent, deadlines missed and opportunities wasted, my frustration turned to despair.

However in the course of writing the book, my mood has changed. I have had such a positive response to the ideas and methods in the book, from people whose experience and judgement I value and trust, that I now believe you *can* succeed in shifting organisational cultures and improving organisations' capability to manage change, provided you follow a balanced, integrated approach. I even found a few success stories to tell!

So thanks to everyone who contributed their enthusiasm and optimism. Here's the 'big idea' we have been talking about.

Background to INPACT

Are you old enough to remember the London Ambulance Service computer fiasco? They introduced a new computer system in the early 90's which was going to really speed up the despatch of ambulances. The new system turned out to be so inefficient that response times actually got worse. In fact, shortly after its introduction, the system failed completely and the service reverted to the previous manual system.

Or were you, like me, forced to change your holiday plans in 1999, because your new passport never arrived? The Home Office permanent secretary was forced to admit that computer problems meant that targets for handling cases would not be met. He said that the introduction of new technology had been expected to lead to cost-reducing staff cuts but had led to such a "set of disasters" that 300 extra officials were now being taken on.

Only last year, the government admitted that while the NHS National Programme for IT had achieved some successes, taken as a whole, it had failed, with only " three wheels still on". Putting it back on track would take "the next decade", not just the next year.

And I have just read the Commons Public Accounts Committee report that called the prison service's C-Nomis programme "a spectacular failure – in a class of its own". This was supposed to give prison and probation officers real-time access to offenders' records but it got so complicated that it never got finished.

These are only the cases that make the headlines. My neighbour's MFI kitchen failed to arrive a few years ago because the company's new inventory system crashed. The £50m system was supposed to improve things for the company but they ended up paying a £30m bill to sort out problems with customer orders and fix the system. They never really recovered from that disaster. Or another example from the private sector: my insurance company failed to send me the documents I needed because their merger with another company had left their systems in a total mess. It took them 3 months to catch up – I didn't ask how much that had cost them.

Why is it that IT-based change projects so often fail to deliver the expected benefits? And what is needed for them to succeed? This was the puzzle that I needed to solve two years ago, while working as a management consultant in the UK public sector. I was aware that many of the modernisation and change projects that I was involved with were not achieving their goals. Take-up of the new processes in the departments was agonisingly slow, the promised efficiency benefits could rarely be proved to have been realised, lots of money was being spent – with often very little to show for it.

This came to a head when, at a meeting to review the status of e-procurement in the public sector, I found that there was widespread agreement among procurement managers that the promised revolution had still not been realised, and that was four years after the first systems had been launched. I wondered why. The usual excuses (lack of time and money) didn't seem to be sufficient. What were the real reasons for this failure? And were they particular to the sector and the type of project?

Apparently not:

In 2008, a McKinsey survey[1] of 3,199 executives around the world found that only one transformation in three succeeds, confirming what John Kotter found back in 1999 when he did the research for his book "Leading Change". And when Harvard Business School tracked the impact of change projects among the Fortune 100 companies, they also found that only 30% of projects produced a positive bottom-line improvement.[2]

Standish Group, an IT industry market research company, carries out an annual survey of project outcomes.[3] Their findings show that project success is rare. In 2009 only 32% of projects succeeded and this was DOWN from previous years (it was 35% in 2004). Their data showed that 24% of projects failed and 44% partially succeeded ("challenged"). Projects over-ran their budgets on average by 45%, their projected delivery times by 63% and they only delivered 67%

[1] 'Creating organizational transformations: McKinsey Global Survey Results', *The McKinsey Quarterly Journal*, August 2008
[2] Nohria, Nitin, 'From the M-form to the N-form: Taking Stock of Changes in the Large Industrial Corporation', Harvard Business School Working Paper, 1996
[3] 'Extreme Chaos', The Standish Group International Inc, 2009

of the expected functionality.

Digging around for further evidence I came across a recent survey of change programmes in over 400 European organisations quoted by Professor John Oakland, Emeritus Professor at Leeds University Business School. He also found that 90% of change programmes faced major implementation problems and only 30% delivered measurable business improvements.

This was worse than I had expected. Surely, if the IT industry and management consultancy companies were aware of these high levels of change project failure, they would be doing everything they could to improve their performance, but when I quoted these statistics to a number of people responsible for project management and efficiency improvement in public and private sector organisations, they only nodded and agreed.

So I started asking people for their take on the problem. I thought I had some of the answers already. My background includes 17 years as a senior manager in BT and 13 years as an independent consultant, including 8 years running a best practice experience-sharing group where major UK companies shared their knowledge and ideas about e-procurement and e-business.

These companies knew that problems arise when there is too much of a focus on the technology, instead of on the business benefits. It's called "technology push". They knew that projects often failed due to poor specification of the systems or the lack of sufficient due diligence on supplier capability. They could quote examples (privately!) of the lack of senior management championship of the project or project managers leaving half-way through an implementation. And they could all point to the inability of system users – that's you and me – to articulate what they need. (Well, how can we, if we don't really understand what the new systems do?)

There was no shortage of reasons for IT-based change projects to fail, or at least to fall short of delivering the expected benefits. But I was not satisfied that these answers were sufficient. Something more was going on, to block change and undermine these projects. After all, we have known about these 'standard' answers for a long time…

I started to read anything and everything published about project failure and uncovered some other common factors in my research:

- Unclear objectives and lack of recognition of the complexity of the project, leading to allocation of inadequate resources to deliver it. So the IT Director *thinks* he has consulted, but ask anyone outside his department, and they will give you a different answer.

- Not enough attention paid to process detail. That can be a killer if, as happened in a large London hospital, the new prescription system didn't have a field on the form for 'possible allergic counter-indications'.

- Old manual processes continuing to be carried out in parallel with the automated ones. Think about it. What is easier: to learn how to input the job request online while dealing with all the non-standard requests that the new system can't handle, or just to carry on doing it all on paper as you always did?

- Lack of attention to training and not enough support for fine-tuning of the new processes and systems to enable realisation of the full benefits. When was the last time you got enough time and support to really learn how a new system worked?

And finally:

- A culture of non-compliance – that's usually the show-stopper!

None of these were 'rocket science', but, together with the 'standard' responses, they came up time and time again. And it didn't seem to matter whether the projects were in the public or private sectors. What they had in common was that the projects were attempting to bring new IT-based systems and modified processes into large, complex and devolved organisations, to improve efficiency and quality of performance.

I looked for a pattern – how did these factors stack up to give me a coherent picture?

I went back to look at all the management science I had acquired over the years, the best practice guides I had researched and written, the models and tools I had come across, inherited, created or adapted along the way, to see whether I could find some answers...

...and what emerged was an underlying idea and a set of models and tools that seemed to fit together and began to answer some of the questions.

I labelled this **INPACT**, which stands for:

INtegrated **P**rocess **A**nd **C**ulture **T**ransformation

'Integrated', because it became clear that the underlying reasons why change and transformation projects do not deliver the expected benefits have to do with how organisations handle both Process *and* Culture. Often the problem is that too much attention is given to the first (Process) and insufficient attention is given to the second (Culture).

Bob Garratt, the management consultant, creates a useful distinction in his book, *The Twelve Organizational Capabilities.*[4]

Here's how he puts it:

"There is a 'soft' side to organisations, which comprises human energies, emotions and learning which...are rarely measured. Yet they affect dramatically organisational effectiveness – the external perception of the organisation by its customers, suppliers and other stakeholders. These 'soft' aspects are the missing key determinants of short-term and long-term organisational capability and performance."

So an organisation's **efficiency** relies on its systems and processes whereas its **effectiveness** comes from its people.

There is an inherent tension between the demands of the organisation's focus on efficiency through systems and processes, and the needs of the individual – the 'culture' or 'people' focus.

I propose to label these: EXTERNAL and INTERNAL. They form two axes, between which a pendulum swings.

---

[4] *The Twelve Organizational Capabilities: Valuing People at Work* – Bob Garratt (1999)

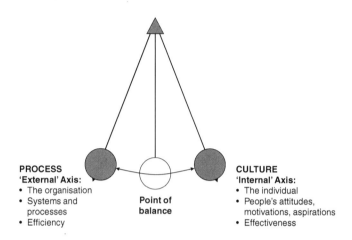

PROCESS		CULTURE
'External' Axis:		'Internal' Axis:
• The organisation		• The individual
• Systems and	**Point of**	• People's attitudes,
processes	**balance**	motivations, aspirations
• Efficiency		• Effectiveness

The point of balance should be mid-way between EXTERNAL and INTERNAL; between 'Process' and 'Culture'; between the organisation, its systems and processes, and the individual, their attitudes, motivations and aspirations.

Because there is an inherent tension between the demands of the organisation and the needs of the individual, between a 'process' view of the world and a 'culture' or 'people' focus, the pendulum swings to the left and right, depending on which force is stronger. It rarely remains for long at the 'point of balance' required to achieve excellent performance. Maintaining balance takes effort and skill. It is fragile and easily disturbed.

One of the main causes of imbalance is change. It requires new systems and processes, new skills and often new people. I will return to the concept of the pendulum. It is a useful way to describe the underlying philosophy behind INPACT, which is that **an integrated and balanced focus on people and process throughout a change or transformation project is essential for success.**

As I started to work with the INPACT models and tools, I noticed something interesting: I was able to use them to carry out quite accurate assessments of an organisation's capability to manage a change project and get the planned results. These assessments didn't take long – just a few days, sometimes only a few hours. INPACT turned out to provide a useful set of insights into the underlying areas of potential failure and the barriers to success.

For example, working with a Business School MBA course to research potential causes of project failure last summer, a simple questionnaire based on the INPACT approach quickly identified real disparities between what project managers were telling us about their projects and what other stakeholders thought about them.

And as part of a post-implementation review of a new system for an NHS Trust, I used INPACT tools to demonstrate that the lack of take-up of the new system was due to an almost complete lack of trust between the clinical and IT people in the organisation.

So I spent some time developing and refining the assessment approach, until I had narrowed it down to just a few key aspects. In an INPACT assessment, each is considered in turn:

First, I look at the **organisation's capability**, including:

- The strength of its organisational culture – attitudes and personal relationships, motivations and habits, aspirations – on the internal axis

- The **business process capability** maturity of the organisation – that's jargon for how consistently and well the organisation manages its routine work – on the external axis.

Then, having assessed the organisation's capability, I look at the **project** – what they are trying to do. This might be a specific change project or an enterprise-wide transformation programme.

I look at four aspects:

1. Clarity of objectives – as I found out in my work with the Business School MBA course, that is often a stumbling block, right at the start.

2. Complexity. So you think your project is simple? Think again. This is often a real eye-opener for even experienced managers.

18

3. The effect of distrust – I didn't believe how absolutely it blocked progress in that NHS Trust.

4. The pull dynamics of benefits realisation. No, I'm not going to explain this – you'll just have to wait and see!

Finally, I include any other factors that may have a significant impact, such as suitability of an IT system or the relationship with partners and other external stakeholders.

So: an organisation's organisational culture + management of its processes = its Capability. What it is trying to do = the Project.

Think of these forming an inverted triangle:

Focusing on the elements in each of these in turn enables me to simplify the task of identifying the factors that really made a difference to project success. I can then integrate them to **quantify the barriers** and understand their potential impact on the bottom-line benefits of the project. So the area between Organisational Capability and The Project in the triangle represents the potential gap between success and failure – a gap that can now be measured. And that's the Change Equation – the 'big idea' that this book is about.

'Objectivising' the risks

Linking the organisational culture model with the other powerful models and tools I have included in INPACT provides a methodology and framework with which to identify the barriers to successful delivery of a change project or programme and to assess the impact these barriers would have, if not dealt with properly, on the costs, timescales and level of benefits realised.

Assuming that the change project is underpinned by a business case (although I have come across a lot that weren't!), the results of this assessment should provide a sufficiently objective output to enable informed discussion about the risks at the planning stages of a project. Why is this important? Because it is vital to persuade entrenched stakeholders to recognise and tackle these risks at an early stage. Leaving it till the project is under way and starting to fall behind schedule – or worse, when it has failed – is much harder and less effective.

Many of these barriers and risks are linked to the underlying culture of the organisation (or part of it, e.g. a department). The expensive failure of the marketing department in a manufacturing company to alert the production team to falling sales trends until it was too late to hold back orders for components arriving at the factory gates, was due in part to the fact that the head of marketing had fallen out with the head of production and they weren't speaking to each other. The inability of a social services department to protect a child, in a recent high-profile case, was not down to the incompetence of the managers and staff. It was due largely to the target-driven culture and the lack of support given to social workers.

A print manager in a large company identified a way to reduce the company's print bills by over 10% and speed up response to requests for print work. It required that the IT department modified a form on the company's intranet so that staff could specify their print requirements in more detail. However this 10-minute job was stuck behind 9 months of other change requests and the print manager could not get the Head of IT to give it priority, despite the potential for savings which, over that 9 months alone would exceed £60,000. The culture in that organisation was such that a personal approach to the Head of IT fell on deaf ears and escalation to a higher level of management led to the print manager being reprimanded!

Attempting to address these cultural issues can often be seen as attacking the emotional identity of senior people in the organisation. So 'objectivising' the barriers to change is the first step to being able to deal with them.

INPACT can be used to change mindsets. And changing mindsets is really the subject of this book!

The INPACT models and tools – your route-map through this book

Here is a quick guide to the way I have set out the ideas and methods that, together, comprise INPACT. (That stands for: Integrated Process and Culture Transformation – just thought I'd remind you!) The book is in four sections:

Section 1: Organisational Capability
Section 2: The Project
Section 3: Delivering Successful Projects
Section 4: Assessment and Implementation

If you are simply interested in understanding the models, you may just wish to scan quickly through the last section. But theory remains just that, until you try to use it. Most 'how to' books are much more interesting when you can apply their insights as go along – and this one is no exception. So I suggest you have a specific project in mind as you read and see what results you get from undertaking an assessment.

SECTION 1: ORGANISATIONAL CAPABILITY

Chapter 2 introduces the **Organisational Culture model** and explain how it works. Chapter 3 describes the nine levels of organisational culture and gives examples.

Chapter 4 focuses on **process** management, the other side of organisational capability and brings into play the **Business Process Capability Maturity** model – a framework well-known to software engineers and one that helps us assess how well an organisation manages its processes.

21

I then bring the two models together in Chapter 5 to create a combined view of the capability of the organisation. This is the organisational capability baseline, against which I can look at the project – in other words, what new things the organisation is trying to bring in and how well it is coping with the changes.

SECTION 2: THE PROJECT

This section starts by looking at the change project itself. First, in Chapter 6, I consider a common factor in many failed projects, the lack of a shared understanding among stakeholders of the objectives of the project.

In Chapter 7, I examine why complexity is often the enemy of success and introduce the Exponential Complexity tool. I have found this a particularly convincing way to change people's assumptions about their project.

Chapter 8 investigates what the real drivers for change are – and introduces the **Change Equation** which was the real starting point for my methodology, hence the title of the book. This is an extremely useful tool.

SECTION 3: DELIVERING SUCCESSFUL PROJECTS

Chapter 9 is all about something apparently quite boring – process mapping and analysis. It may not be very exciting, but actually, the lack of **process visibility** is where a lot of projects stumble. The best projects I have come across have used process mapping to involve the end users of the new processes – the people who count – in inventing their own route-map to the future.

22

The focus on process until this point made a simplistic assumption; that you can improve the way you do things by designing and managing your processes better. That is true for routine processes, but what do you do about processes that are not routine? Chapter 10 looks at how to identify and deal with non-routine work.

Another key barrier to success, as I have already signalled, is the lack of trust between people in many organisations. Chapter 11 reveals the **Trust/Cost** relationship. Sounds interesting – and it is! This chapter is also where I bring in the often difficult topic of what to do about external stakeholders.

There is always resistance to change, but it seems to be greater when you introduce technology – why is that? I have a go at getting to grips with this question – and what to do about it – in Chapter 12.

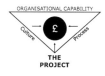

Selecting the right technology and good suppliers to help you implement it can be critical to a change project's success. Chapter 13 suggests five key questions to ask.

I promised that I would explain what the 'pull dynamics of benefits realisation' actually means and Chapter 14 is where I do that with the **Dynamic Benefits Realisation** model – a very powerful catalyst for change.

SECTION 4: ASSESSMENT AND IMPLEMENTATION
This section is where I bring these models and tools together to offer

Map Organisational Capability	Develop capability/ complexity indicator	Measure trust, check for BRP & other key factors	Calculate impact on business case, share results	Develop Route Map, implement Action Plan

a practical toolkit to improve the success of your change projects.

Chapter 15 sets out a typical assessment and deals with how to quantify the barriers and apply the findings to a business case.

In most instances, it's the organisation's capability to handle change that needs attention in order to improve the outcome of change projects, so Chapter 16 looks at how to use the organisational culture model to develop a Route-Map to drive up the organisation's capability.

In Chapter 17 I suggest how to use all this data to develop an Action Plan to overcome the barriers to successful change.

Appendices: I have included a fully worked example of an assessment for reference at Appendix A, and have gathered together some of the other examples used throughout the book into short case studies for easy reference at Appendix B.

Who should use INPACT?

I have had a number of conversations with **project managers** who started by claiming that their projects are delivered on time and to budget and realise their planned benefits. When you quiz them, it usually turns out that this is a pretty unrealistic picture, but even then, they will tell you that the projects that didn't succeed (most of them) fell short for reasons that had nothing to do with them – the senior manager sponsoring the project left, circumstances changed, budgets were cut etc.

I have found that it is usually unprofitable to suggest to project managers that there is a better way, one that within a few days, and for a very low cost, would:

- Identify barriers to success in a planned project.
- Predict how these will impact on benefits.
- Quantify true costs and timescales of the project.
- Recommend the actions that need to be included to ensure success.
- Help to ensure that the key stakeholders (e.g. project sponsor, senior management budget-holders etc) recognise the issues and are on board with the need to address them.

I have had more success getting through to **senior management** stakeholders, such as finance directors, who appreciate, right away, the tangible outcomes of the assessment and the way it facilitates an objective dialogue at Board level to ensure that sufficient resources are included in the project plan to deal with the barriers.

Another group who like what INPACT can do are the **IT solution and service providers**. They know that a good year is when more of their client projects come in on time, within budget and deliver the planned benefits. That means they make a profit on the work, have the opportunity for on-sell with the client and can use the project as a sales case study. A bad year is when more of their client projects are delayed, overspent and don't succeed in delivering expected benefits. Profits go out of the window, no on-sell and no reference case studies. Most years are just on one side or the other of the WIN-LOSE divide but sometimes a project that goes badly can set them back years.

So what is the secret behind consistent profits for a solution and service provider? I would suggest it is:

- Understanding the risks and getting the client to understand them too, before agreeing the contract.
- Knowing what needs doing within the project – and outside it – to mitigate the risks and getting the client to do his part in ensuring success.

Using the INPACT models and tools can help to do both of these by providing an objective assessment for discussion at the start.

For both senior managers and their suppliers, I am really advocating the use of INPACT as a **due diligence** tool, to supplement whatever methods are used at present. This becomes even more critical when planning a merger or acquisition, when it is essential to understand the cultural differences and capability maturity of both organisations. There are few other methodologies around that will help you to assess and benchmark these 'soft' aspects, quickly and objectively. The same is true for venture capitalists wanting to invest in a company. Failure to spot the weaknesses in the company's capability to manage change will seriously jeopardise the return on their investment.

Finally, INPACT can contribute significantly to the development of **collaborative and partnering** ways of working. Government is increasingly demanding that UK public sector organisations move to collaborative and shared service working, in response to the relentless pressure to 'do more for less' and to become more 'citizen-centric'. Collaborative working and shared services provision is extremely challenging to even the best managed organisations. A key consideration is whether the culture and business process capability of each of the partnering organisations is sufficiently mature to accommodate the transition and operation of an effective collaboration or shared service. It is rare that this is considered in an objective, quantified way. The government's Gateway Review process, for example, doesn't include these aspects.

When to use INPACT

Clearly, the best time to use INPACT is before the start of a project. If you apply the assessment tools when scoping the project and building the business case, you can avoid overspend and delay and reduce the risk that benefits don't come up to expectations. Having identified the barriers to success at the start of a project and put in place actions to deal with them, you should be able to introduce key elements of process transformation and culture change that will ensure a successful project.

Re-applying the assessment tools during the course of a project or programme will allow you to track and calibrate progress objectively, which will help you to adjust your programme and sustain its momentum. It should also allow you to manage any unrealistic expectations and maintain users' commitment to making the changes that will deliver the benefits.

What if the results of this assessment show little or no progress? Or the project is not delivering the desired changes? The methodology should enable you to establish and bring out the underlying roots of the problem/s and work with the key stakeholders to develop an action plan to deal with these. Using the relevant INPACT tools, you will be able to engage and turn around the key 'blockers' of progress and support your ongoing implementation programme to a successful conclusion.

And finally

The methodology described in this book is deliberately high-level and intended to enable an organisation to assess whether a project is likely to succeed in delivering the expected benefits, on time and within budget. It is *not* meant to replace in-depth analysis nor the application of professional project and change management tools. But it will indicate where these are needed.

I have used a number of examples in the book, drawn from my experience and that of people – both clients and colleagues – with whom I have been discussing the principles of INPACT. The stories are there to reinforce a point, so will have been simplified – undoubtedly, the real life situations were far more complex.

Unless that information has already been the subject of a published article, I have not revealed my sources or the names of the organisations involved. I know that my peers in management literature like name-dropping, but confidentiality was usually a condition for revealing the worst horror stories.

You are welcome to adopt and adapt these models and tools, as I have done; feel free to use them to improve the outcomes of your projects, but do please acknowledge your sources and check with me before republishing any of these materials.

SECTION 1: ORGANISATIONAL CAPABILITY

2

Organisational Culture model

In these times of economic upheaval, change is inevitable – it's being forced on all of us. The last thing we need is for change projects to fail. But the evidence is that reorganisations often fail to deliver real improvement in performance. A CIPD report surveyed 800 executives and put this at 40% of cases[5] and as I mentioned in the introduction, other research suggests that 30% of change initiatives fail to deliver their intended result.

Although the primary focus for most managers involved in delivering change and transformation is on the project or programme, in practice how well they plan and implement the project may *not* be what dictates how successful the project turns out to be in delivering the desired benefits. Often it rests as much on the capability of the organisation to cope with change and take advantage of new systems, particularly where these cut across the organisation's traditional structural and cultural boundaries.

Here's an example: A Local Authority was spending £200m each year on goods and services and decided to introduce an e-procurement portal to put the council's contracts online and improve efficiency.

---

[5] 'Reorganising for success: CEOs and HR Managers' perceptions' – CIPD Survey 2003

Unfortunately, the Finance department wasn't prepared to change the antiquated financial accounting system and the suppliers of that system wanted an unreasonable amount of money to develop the interface with the e-procurement portal, so the objective of end-to-end paper-free transactions was not achievable.

Worse, the managers in the service departments decided that as the system did not deal with some of their more complex service requirements, it would be given low priority, so the number of service users never grew beyond a handful. With this low user take-up, suppliers were reluctant to sign up to the portal, so the system only featured a small number of office commodities suppliers. That in turn dampened user interest in logging on and the system fell into disuse.

This example (described further in Appendix A) shows how important it is to pay attention to the way that people interact with the organisation – the organisational culture of the organisation. In fact it is one of the most important secrets of success in delivering a transformation project. This chapter will describe the model I have adopted and developed to bring out the fundamental principles underpinning any organisational culture and understand the dynamics of the interaction between the individual and the organisation. Later on in the book I will describe some of the ways to use this model to help you shift the dominant organisational culture and implement change.

Any two organisations working in the same field and delivering similar goods or services to the same customers will have their own way of doing things, their unique culture, which, if ignored, will undermine any attempt to implement change and modernisation.

For example, a social housing organisation (a not-for-profit 'company' set up to take over the management of housing stock from a council) was being tasked by government to develop collaborative working with seven other social housing organisations in their area, in order to share costs, leverage buying power and raise the quality of housing management. The CEO was concerned that the other organisations had different styles of management and might have lower levels of capability.

Analysis confirmed that the CEO had achieved a closer alignment of the needs and aspirations of his staff with those of the company, compared to a more bureaucratic culture in the other housing associations. An open-door policy meant that trust was high in his company, whereas groups in the other companies tended to keep information to themselves and only communicated upwards by means of formal reports.

So the CEO was right to be concerned. He recognised that he and his managers had developed a different approach, a different way of thinking and a different set of values from those in the other companies – a different organisational culture. The stronger this cultural difference, the more difficult it is to share and collaborate.

You don't have to look outside the walls of most large organisations to see how different groups and departments have developed their own cultures. Underlying and driving this cultural divide are the two potentially conflicting forces that I briefly referred to in the introduction: 1) the individual and his/her needs and aspirations; 2) the organisation and how it operates. The weaker the organisation's culture, the more that the individuals influence these local cultures. And the weaker the influence of the CEO, in general, the weaker the organisation's culture.

Around 15 years ago, a management consultant named Warren Kinston published a framework[6] for describing approaches to decision-making and showed how they fitted together in an evolutionary model of organisational cultures. This identified the tension between the individual and the organisation as a fundamental factor. (Our pendulum, remember?)

The tension between the individual and the organisation is inherent in the Total Quality Management (TQM) continuous improvement model and many of the change management models in use over the years, but none of them have brought it out as a fundamental underlying principle, which, of course, it is.

I saw in Warren's model the basis for an idea. If the effectiveness

---

[6] *Strengthening the Organisational Culture: Phasing the Transformation of Organizations* – Warren Kinston (1994)

33

of an organisation depended on the extent to which it was able to bring these forces into alignment, why not explore the cultural barriers to success using this framework?

Note that I have only loosely borrowed Warren's model as the basis for the INPACT culture analysis. I have not followed his very precise thinking, nor adhered precisely to his terminology or methodology. I make no apology for this. His is a far more empirical approach; mine, I hope, an eminently pragmatic one. [7]

Warren's model was in the shape of an evolutionary spiral, with each style building on the previous styles. Why a spiral? Well, have a look at this illustration.

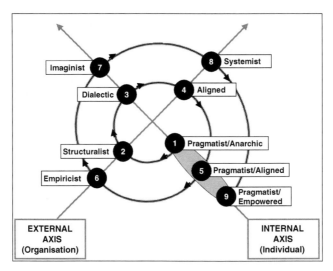

Source: adapted from 'Strengthening the Organisational Culture: Phasing the Transformation of Organizations' – Warren Kinston 1994

Each of the styles on the left-to-right EXTERNAL axis focuses on the organisation and its EXTERNAL or organisational responses,

---

[7] Warren Kinston has taken this work much further forward, and has proposed that if we look carefully around us, there is a natural Taxonomy of Human Elements in our Endeavours (THEE). The decision-making and organisational culture studies are small but typical parts of THEE: http://sites.google.com/site/introducingtheeonline/

while each of the styles on the right-to-left INTERNAL axis focuses on the individuals within the organisation and their INTERNAL responses.

See how the pendulum moves from the INTERNAL axis to the EXTERNAL axis and back again, kept in motion by the tension between them. It is rising as it swings – each style building on the last one, not replacing it.

The important insight that I took from Kinston's diagram was this: in order to progress up the management evolution spiral, we have to recognise and fully deal with the underlying tension between the individual (INTERNAL responses) playing a meaningful role in the organisation and the organisation (EXTERNAL responses) which uses people to succeed. In INPACT I have used this spiral model to identify the dominant management style as a powerful indicator of how well the organisation will cope with change. I also use the model to develop the route-map that an organisation needs to follow to become culturally more mature and capable of empowering its people to deliver higher levels of performance.

In the next Chapter, I will go into each of the organisational culture styles in some detail, but first let's have a canter through how the model works and the different styles it describes.

How the Organisational Culture model works

We all start by doing everything ourselves, whether it's a new business or a task force in a larger organisation = **Pragmatist/Anarchic culture.**
This works for a while, but as our organisation grows, we need to develop a structure and delegate. If that doesn't happen, the efficiency of the organisation declines. Either all the power resides with one person and nothing gets done, or anarchy reigns and nobody knows what is happening.

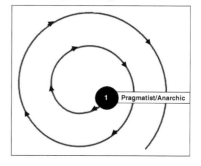

In a large organisation, there may be pockets of Pragmatist/

Anarchic culture, where a group has been allowed to develop a level of autonomy from the rest of the organisation and does things its own way. These are usually the most difficult groups to influence and to move to new ways of working.

Most organisations have evolved rules and processes to manage their activity = **Structuralist culture**. The problem with the Structuralist culture is that, over time, it can become bureaucratic and 'tribal'. At this stage many organisations bring in the consultants, reorganise and restructure, bringing in new systems and streamlining their processes, but this skips an important step (see Dialectic culture below).

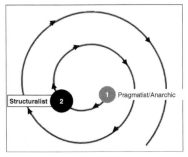

The focus on restructuring and process improvement leads to a **Rationalist culture**, which is supposed to bring efficiency – the trouble is, 're-engineering' processes doesn't seem to work very well. Why? Well perhaps we didn't spend enough time gaining the ownership for the changes. Unless people understand the reasons why things have to change and are brought into the process, they will resist it. So let's go back and look at where that happens…

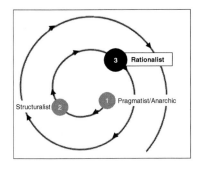

Organisations that have achieved a more consultative, sharing approach will have moved from a structuralist culture to a **Dialectic culture** (dialectic = dialogue). This harnesses the informal networking that people do naturally, by encouraging it and making it part of the 'way we do

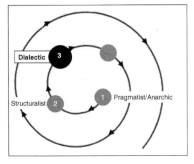

things'. Social and peer networks become the way the information is exchanged and how people identify who has the knowledge and skills to help them with a problem or task.

Now that the aspirations and motivation of the individual are aligned with the policies of the organisation, the progression is to an **Aligned culture.**

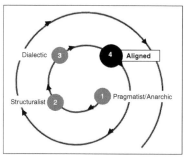

This is the goal of many models for organisational quality improvement, such as TQM. It is based on the simple premise that if everyone is pulling in the same direction, the energy that used to be dissipated in in-fighting can now be used more productively to improve quality.

When everyone is pulling in the same direction, we can relax the rules, give people more control over how they achieve results = **Pragmatist culture** again, only this time it's not anarchic, as it was in the first cycle, but **Pragmatist/Aligned.**

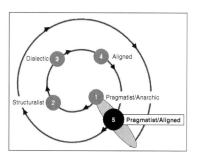

Now that the organisation is working as a team, communication can flow undistorted, across functions as well as up and down – so management decisions can be better informed and the organisation can focus on the real world outside itself = **Empiricist culture.**

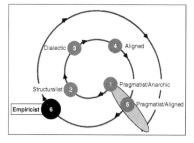

A manager in an organisation with an Empiricist culture has the information to make radical 'leaps of faith' and innovative decisions. That requires a different calibre of manager and an **Imaginist**

culture which values innovation and improvement.

Once the organisation is working as well as this, the captain at the helm can stop fire-fighting and intervening and start navigating = **Systemist culture**.

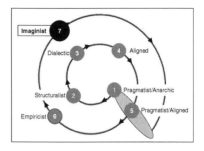

Finally, I come back to where we started, Pragmatist, but with the individual now being fully supported by visionary management and empowered to make key decisions = **Pragmatist/ Empowered culture**.

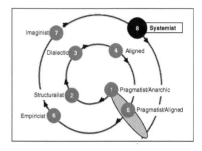

That was a quick skate through the Organisational Culture model. In the next chapter I take a closer look at each management style in turn. As you read the descriptions and examples, consider which management style – or styles – most accurately describes your organisation (or your part of it).

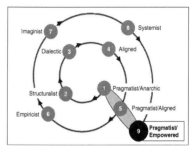

3

Mapping Your Organisational Culture – the Nine Levels

Level 1: Pragmatic/Anarchic

In an organisation dominated by a Pragmatic/Anarchic culture, it's

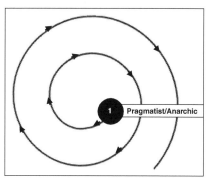

the results that count. Management is arms-length and rewards success, so individual members of the team are left to do more or less what they like, as long as they achieve results.

There are some laid-down procedures, but people only follow them or take up a new initiative if they see benefits for themselves in doing so. In this culture, the individual is more important than the team.

That's fine if performance is stimulated by internal competition and bonuses, but it is not a good culture for an organisation that needs to respond to new threats and opportunities by making rapid changes to its business model and instigating wholesale improvements in efficiency.

A good example is the NHS Trust whose culture has jeopardised the success of all transformational initiatives. This includes poor alignment between clinical and managerial groups, a disinclination on the part of medical consultants to follow the CEO's lead and a lack of shared systems and knowledge flow across departments. In some cases this pragmatic/anarchic culture has led to poor take-up of new systems and a lower than planned level of benefits from improvements, but in other instances, projects simply failed – diminishing, rather than increasing the Trust's performance.

A Pragmatic/anarchic organisational culture is one where the individual (INTERNAL) response to the world of work dominates. In my own company, if I don't get up in the morning, it's me I have to kick. And I get all the kudos for a successful project. That style suits small, dynamic businesses. It does not suit a larger organisation. For that, one has to swing the pendulum across to the Structuralist management style.

Level 2: Structuralist

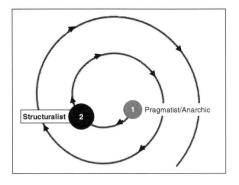

An organisation with a dominant Structuralist culture uses rules and procedures to function. If you work in a large corporate or public sector organisation you will recognise this environment. Work is managed and rewarded according to laid-down policies and targets which are translated into devolved authorities, procedures and measures so that everyone knows exactly where they are and what they have to do. Structure is useful – it allows organisations to scale up activity and not lose control. It brings predictability and consistency to work carried out by a lot of people, sometimes in multiple locations across the country or the world.

But after a time, the rules and procedures can start to become barriers to change rather than facilitators of efficiency. The organisation can become over-bureaucratic, with 'silo working' hindering the sharing of ideas and knowledge across groups and departments.

'Silo working' is a useful shorthand. It's an excellent description for the way people working in a Structuralist culture tend to focus inwards, at local group or department level and see other groups and departments as 'them'. This is a natural response – our loyalties and relationships will always be predominantly with those immediately around us, unless the job and the organisation provides the incentives, opportunities and avenues to extend our horizons.

The walls and fences we build around us in life are intended to stop others being able to come in and take what is ours. They also slow down our own responses to the outside world – we can choose whether to respond or pretend we didn't hear. Internal 'walls and fences' between group and departments are just as effective. Simply by naming the role of a person we put boundaries around them – what they can and cannot do, who they report to and who reports to them and, in many organisations, the size and location of their office.

Most organisations will have at least some silos, where the focus is inward-looking and most communication is vertical; where managers act as 'information gatekeepers', making it difficult to obtain information across departmental boundaries; where improving efficiency becomes an uphill battle and close working relationships with external customers, partners and suppliers is downright impossible. In such organisations, you will find part-duplicated data being held in six different databases across departments but nobody

41

will be able to give you a straight answer to a simple question.

Silo working is the predominant cultural characteristic in many of the examples I have come across where projects have failed. The effect of this compartmentalised, defensive and, in corporate terms, 'selfish' behaviour is always negative and can be destructive. People in a Structuralist style organisation may be less willing to put themselves out to help others achieve corporate goals, because they have insulated themselves from those goals.

The information you need to perform effectively may not be available because others haven't seen your need as a priority. What top management knows is governed by the way that information flows, and that is likely to be channelled via the hierarchical structure.

A Structuralist culture does not encourage sharing of information with other parts of the organisation – indeed, in the worst examples I have come across, internal departments are seen as the enemy!

A multi-national pharmaceutical company saved 30% on a £15k spend by employing an innovative approach to source and produce a branded promotional item. The consultant who helped them identify this approach is tearing out his hair with frustration – he recognised that by using the same approach across the whole company, they could save at least £250k every year, just in the UK. But there is no-one to approach with this offer – every department does its own buying, makes its own decisions, finds its own suppliers. The level of competition between departments is such that opportunities like this to make savings across the organisation are not shared. Internal communication is top-down, so unless he can get 'air-time' with the Finance Director or CEO, he cannot sell his solution – and the company will continue to miss opportunities like this.

Extend this lack of communication to the relationship between Board members and critical decisions don't get made. That deterioration can even breed conflict between Board members, which causes the organisation to focus on internal power-play, causing it to lose sight of its customers and the competition.

So change in a Structuralist organisation is slow, often blocked by 'selfish' behaviour and when decisions are made, they are often

imposed from above, with superficial but inadequate consultation.
Local Councils are typically prone to the negative characteristics of a Structuralist organisational culture: large, devolved multi-site, multi-department service organisations, in which distinct tribal cultures have been allowed to develop within departments and specialist groups. Senior management are reluctant or unable to impose mandatory change beyond their own domains and information does not flow readily across the organisation – knowledge is power. As a result, strategic thinking becomes detached from the day-to-day operation of the organisation, critical decisions are often late and poorly communicated and an interventionist, fire-fighting style of management becomes the norm. The pressure on everyone in the organisation and the number of changes imposed on them over the years has taken its toll and any new initiative to improve efficiency is resisted.

I wrote in the introduction about the manager responsible for an in-house print department who was reprimanded for trying to get a form changed, in order to save over £60,000. The silo culture and level of distrust in that organisation was such that it over-rode common sense and the best interests of the company.

It is worth looking at what happens when a Pragmatic/Anarchic culture meets a Structuralist management style. This happened when a small but fast-growing and innovative company was acquired by a larger organisation. When I became involved, both had been experiencing real problems adapting and accommodating the culture and processes of the other.

The larger company had a strong Structuralist culture. Management decisions were passed down with no more than a formal 'tick-box' consultation process and change took forever. The smaller company was heavily focused on achieving bottom line profit and individual members of the team worked together to hit their targets, but otherwise 'did their own thing'. Corporate policies and procedures were kept to a minimum and were often ignored.

Managers and staff in both organisations were told about the merger, not consulted. This made little impact on managers in the larger company, which began imposing its way of working on the new combined organisation. However performance in the division formed by the smaller company took a nose-dive and some key people left rather than comply with the new culture.

This is a classic situation where the cultures and capabilities of the two organisations are incompatible and where, unless remedial steps are taken quite quickly, the opportunity will evaporate for them to create something greater than the sum of its parts.

The Structuralist culture suits a stable environment where consistency, precision and strict adherence to rules is required to achieve performance. How many organisations function in that kind of environment? In today's world, the pace of change has quickened, uncertainty and complexity have replaced stability and simplicity and Structuralist organisations find themselves unable to respond.

So what can one do to improve the performance of a Structuralist-dominated organisation? The typical response has been 'process re-engineering' or 'process improvement' initiatives, redesigning and streamlining the business processes, cutting out obstacles and speeding up the flow of information and decision-making. As you will see, that is not the answer.

Level 3: Dialectic

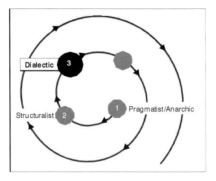

The Organisational Culture pendulum is swinging. From Structuralist it swings around to Dialectic. What is that to do with addressing the problems I described arising from the Structuralist culture?

The term Dialectic means using dialogue to get results. The

pendulum has swung back over to the INTERNAL axis, focusing on the individual within the structured organisation. An organisation that has adopted a Dialectic management style puts a high value on the individual and on sharing knowledge, as opposed to having (and protecting) knowledge. In a Structuralist culture, the emotional 'climate' is such that strategic knowledge gives people organisational power, while managers and staff in a Dialectic culture are rewarded for networking and exchanging ideas and information, breaking down any barriers between them.

As a result, silo working is not a significant barrier to change. Lines of communication are freed up, energy is not diverted to hiding mistakes or grumbling about what is wrong but doing nothing about it. People feel respected and are involved and consulted when changes are needed.

A key characteristic of a Dialectic style of management is the use of 'who you know' to solve problems, as opposed to relying just on 'what you know'. This becomes a key strength when dealing with non-routine work, as I will discuss in Chapter 10.

So the walls and fences are starting to come down. A culture of trust and respect is growing, bringing with it the ability of individuals to perceive and be motivated by more than local loyalties.

I came across a good example of a strong Dialectic culture – but unfortunately only after it had been destroyed. A civil service organisation which was responsible for developing and communicating government policy had, over the years, developed their approach to the mix of routine report-writing punctuated by urgent and last-minute requests for vital and often high-profile information and expert opinion.

The managers and staff had created a strong network of contacts across and outside the organisation. This gave them the ability to find the information they needed quickly to respond effectively to the Minister or the press.

The networks were sustained informally and socially, as well as in more conventional ways – so lunches with experts and influencers were recognised as important opportunities to build one's network, as well as attending public conferences and scheduled office meetings; drinks in the pub after formal internal meetings were as valuable – perhaps more so – than the work done in the meetings...

It sounds rather laid back and unmanaged – the stereotype of the civil servant of old: short hours, long lunches and a casual approach to deadlines, but people in this organisation worked long hours, took work home and got things done quickly, quietly and very effectively. The director of the organisation was very visible, attending groups and meetings and always accessible. He was well liked and respected and trusted his team, so change was relatively painless and they adapted well to the onset of new technologies, such as web-based communication and the increased speed of response that this demanded.

All this came to an end when the organisation was absorbed into a larger central government department. The key people, including the director, were reassigned different roles, rendering their informal networks irrelevant and ineffective. Social networking was discouraged and all compilation, communication and storage of knowledge had to adhere to strict rules and use shared data systems – supposedly so that Ministers and the Press Office could access the information they needed more readily.

Needless to say, it didn't work! The organisation suffered badly from its 'corporate loss of memory' and never recovered its former effectiveness. When I visited them, it was startling how quickly the Dialectic culture had been replaced by a lack of trust, poor communication of important information and a clear loss of motivation to achieve results (now expressed as performance targets).

However I must add a note of warning. A Dialectic style can be very effective, but it can also become undisciplined and unless properly managed, a way to get around formal processes. Against that last example could be set many stories of organisations which were just not properly and well managed, where the lunches were more important than the meetings, where people spent more time talking than doing... What is required is a balance, which is the essence of the INPACT approach.

Level 4: Aligned

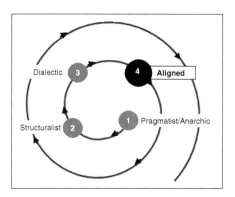

Before I describe the Aligned culture, a word about its 'poor relation', the Rationalist culture, which inhabits the same space in the organisational culture spiral.

Remember that the pendulum is swinging between INTERNAL and EXTERNAL, between the needs and aspirations of the individual and those of the organisation. The Dialectic culture is heavily over on the INTERNAL side – focusing on the individual, ensuring that each member of the team feels respected and listened to. As the pendulum swings back to the EXTERNAL axis, the focus shifts to shine the spotlight on the way the organisation manages itself, its formal policies and processes.

As I mentioned earlier, there was for many years a fashion in management consultancy for process re-engineering. This was seen as the answer to the need for increased efficiency and improved performance. "Let's get rid of the slow, bureaucratic ways of working by streamlining and rationalising the processes". The problem was that it didn't work.

By concentrating too heavily on improving processes, those responsible lost sight of the need to involve the people in the organisations who were using the existing processes, to harness their creativity and to allow them to work out the best ways to cope with the changes. After all, this was where the most detailed knowledge lay. By ignoring them and insisting on process maps and models with

47

fancy names, the 'experts' lost sight of the balanced approach needed to bring about change. To paraphrase Bob Garratt's definition in 'The Twelve Organizational Capabilities', they got efficiency but not effectiveness.

In the vocabulary of our model, process re-engineering is moving along the EXTERNAL axis, rather than swinging from INTERNAL to EXTERNAL and back again. What is needed for the focus on rationalisation of process to be effective is that the organisation has a strong Dialectic culture. Then – and only then – will the redesign of the organisation's processes be informed by the individual's desire to align him/herself with the corporate priorities and goals. Rationalist becomes Aligned.

So to the Aligned style of management. This describes a culture in which people are pointing in the same direction to achieve tasks and have the emotional commitment to a set of shared values which determine how they work. Typically, as one would expect, this is found in organisations with a good level of interaction across boundaries. It is usually characterised also by strong, inspirational leadership. Rules and processes are still needed, but the values and aspirations of the staff in these organisations are in line with the policies and strategic direction of the organisation, rather than being in conflict with them.

When people feel valued and understand how they fit into the scheme of things, they are more motivated to accept rules and comply with them. They recognise the need for changes that will benefit the organisation, even if these do not reduce their own workload or help them achieve their own targets.

One of the best Aligned organisations I have ever come across is a small charity that employs only a handful of managers and administrative staff, but has a large number of volunteers who represent the real 'workforce'. Tapping into the energy and motivation of these volunteers is not the problem – the challenge is containing this energy and motivation, keeping them all pointing in the same direction and ensuring they use the systems and procedures that allow the charity to maintain a low overhead cost.

The way the charity has dealt with this was to create a 'flat' management structure, bringing people together to develop good ways of working that suits them, letting people come together in small task force groups to develop new solutions to problems and opportunities. The trust that is generated by these activities permeates the way the charity runs its day-to-day operations. Everyone understands the 'greater good' rationale for changes and accepts that these may not always benefit them, but they are constantly looking for ways to improve their own contribution and will expect others to support any changes that would enable this to become more effective.

This alignment leads to an important step-change in culture which can differentiate a successful organisation from one that is struggling to achieve its aims. Before I follow the pendulum on its course, I thought it would be salutary to quote an example of a large financial services company that acquired a rival organisation and tried to merge the two.

Over the years, the parent company had developed a very rigid Structuralist culture; the target organisation culture was Aligned and strongly Dialectic – managers consulted and trusted their staff, who felt valued and well-informed. Information was shared informally as well as at more formal meetings, so top management knew what their staff thought about issues. The parent company admired its rival, which out-performed them on all fronts and when the opportunity arose to acquire them, there was no question – it was the right move.

However, when the two companies merged, the decision was made to move similar departments and functions together into the same building and get rid of managers and staff that were no longer needed. Although the top management in the target company survived the merger, many of their colleagues did not. How did the resulting teams come out in a subsequent assessment?

Predictably, the Structuralist culture dominated throughout the new organisation. The merger had not just undermined the Aligned ways of working, it had bred serious problems of poor relationships and lack of trust which acted to embed the 'silo' culture and which would take years to overcome. This was reflected in the poor market performance of the merged company and a disastrous set of customer satisfaction results.

So the Aligned culture is rather fragile. It needs to sit on a foundation comprising the best of the earlier organisational cultures. The challenge for leaders and managers is to create the 'climate', rules and reward structures to achieve alignment. Confronted by a strong Structuralist culture, it will dissipate, as people start looking after their own interests and stop sharing information. This characteristic applies even more to the next culture: Pragmatic/Aligned.

Level 5: Pragmatic/Aligned

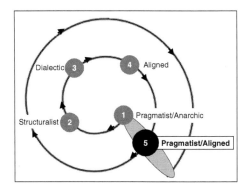

Once the people in the organisation are working in an aligned culture, there is the opportunity to reduce the level of supervision and micro-management that is a characteristic of a Structuralist culture. Rather than depending on targets imposed by the system, you can start to encourage people to develop their own targets. This does not work in a Pragmatic/Anarchic culture, as everyone would pull in different directions, creating chaos and impacting on the organisation's ability to achieve anything. And obviously you could not achieve this in an organisation dominated by a Structuralist culture. But in an Aligned culture, self-generated targets become a possibility and these are recognised to be far more effective than any objectives you impose on people.

The culture in a Pragmatic/Aligned organisation is action-focused. The management structure is likely to be 'flat' with a minimum of hierarchies. People are expected to get on and achieve high quality results with the minimum of management supervision.

But unlike Pragmatic/Anarchic, where the focus is on results at almost any cost, the culture now encourages people to be more corporately responsible, working as a team rather than as individuals.

Managers in a Pragmatic/Aligned organisation trust their staff to act in the best interests of the organisation, so apply a more hands-off style of management and supervision. This means that decisions are devolved and made by people closer to the customer, allowing a faster and more appropriate response – a key to success and growth in a business and vital to providing a good quality of service in public sector organisations.

Another characteristic of the best examples of an organisation working in a Pragmatic/Aligned management style is the way the organisation deals with the inevitable consequence of devolving responsibility – mistakes. These are seen as opportunities to learn and share knowledge, rather than opportunities to blame and reprimand. "Of course I let people make mistakes," one manager in an organisation with a predominantly Pragmatic/Aligned culture told me. "It's how we all learn".

The 'no-blame' culture is perhaps the most noticeable feature of one company that had succeeded in evolving its management style to embrace a Pragmatic/Aligned culture. I was talking to one of the managers and asked how he was doing. "Fine", he replied. "My project has just been closed down." My expression obviously showed what I was thinking… how could that be fine? Didn't it mean he was for the chop? Not at all, he explained. *He* was the one who had gone to the management board with the figures. *He* had recommended that they move out of the sector. It was *his* decision, backed by his board, to close down the project. So what was he doing now? "Oh, there are a couple of positions in other projects that I am considering – and I may be in line for a Head of Division role".

The company had rightly recognised that the mistake was a corporate mistake and were not planning to shoot the messenger. Quite the opposite: they recognised his role in seeing the need to withdraw from the unprofitable sector quickly and at low cost. He was being rewarded for saving the company a lot of money and future problems.

This ability to read the signs and take appropriate and timely action can be the single factor that differentiates a successful company from one that plods along. However it requires accurate and up-to-date information. The next chapter follows the pendulum back across to the EXTERNAL axis, where it will become clear how important this is – the Empiricist culture.

Level 6: Empiricist

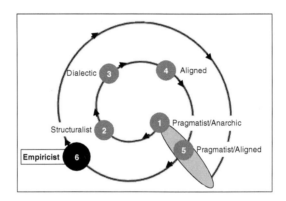

Good quality information about the 'real world' is vital to any organisation. In order to be useful, it needs to be collected and analysed quickly and to be distributed across departments as well as up and down the management hierarchy. It must not get delayed or distorted on the way, as it would in a Structuralist culture, passing through departmental silos. If the information is timely and accurate, management can make decisions that are well-informed and effective.

An Empiricist culture recognises the importance of 'real world' information. It encourages people to monitor what is happening in its market or sphere of activity. Staff are not barred from access to the Internet. Managers do not query proposals to spend money on journals and conferences and the staff who read and attend these are expected to circulate any information that they think others might be interested in.

The Empiricist culture can only thrive in an organisation that has been built upon the best aspects of all the previous cultures. People know where they fit into the organisation's structure; they take responsibility for setting and achieving goals. They have extensive networks within and outside the organisation so they can quickly locate someone who knows where to find information or who has the skills they need. Their managers are not insulated by walls and fences. They are visible and accessible. And they understand the dangers of an inward-facing style of management.

When, a few years ago, Sony acquired MGM, the story went around that the American consultants advised the 'old men' at the head of Sony to leave the US corporate structure in place, allow the US managers to continue defining their own strategy and direction and develop a hands-off corporate relationship. They explained that the US corporate culture was quite different from that in Japan, which has a strong 'command and obey' culture and where employee loyalty was taken for granted. They advised that a typical US employee changed jobs and companies several times in their career – and this was particularly true in a media sector company. Any attempt to introduce a Japanese management style into the company would result in the loss of its people and consequent drop in performance.

But that advice fell on deaf ears. The 'old men', insulated by the command and obey culture of their own company, sent over a team of managers, threw out long-established methods of working which had been evolved over time to be effective in the US market and imposed a tight regime that reported directly into the parent company. Within three months, all the key people at MGM had left and it took several years before Sony MGM recovered.

I don't know how much of this story is apocryphal, but it's a brilliant example of the national and regional cultural groupings that affect the behaviour of organizations. Geert Hofstede famously identified how these major differences between national cultures influence business behaviour[8].

You don't have to look as far to see similar differences between organisations in this country. An organisation that is able to use information well is bound to be more successful. This is reinforced as I swing the pendulum across to the INTERNAL axis and look at how managers benefit from working in this environment.

Level 7: Imaginist

I have come to a management style which is particularly close to my heart, the Imaginist culture. As I moved through my career, first in

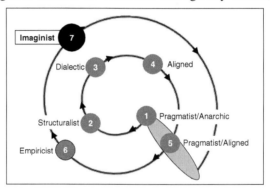

British Telecom, then working in a consultancy, I noticed that most managers were so busy micro-managing, they didn't seem to have time to sit back and think. 'Thinking time' became something I learned to prize and to make time for, however frantic the schedule. Another thing that bothered me was that I never felt I had the information I needed to make decisions quickly enough to impact significantly on a project's success. So when I set up on my own, my ambition was to work with entrepreneurs and smaller companies at the conceptual stage of a project, to imagine the future, collect the information needed to develop a structured plan to get them there and then help them make it happen.

---

[8] Hofstede, Geert – *Culture's Consequences: comparing values, behaviors, institutions, and organizations across nations* (2001)

History is full of good intentions and mine were overtaken by events. I was asked to carry out some work for a Local Authority, which led to other work and soon I was an expert in modernisation of public sector systems... Suffice it to say I never did manage to establish myself primarily as a consultant who works with entrepreneurs and smaller companies! However, the name I came up with for my consultancy company did stick: The Imaginist Company. The Imaginist thinks outside the box, is open to new ideas and collects information avidly about everything. The Imaginist is a strategist, a dreamer and a visionary, but also a pragmatist, keen to get on and do – keen to make a difference.

In an Imaginist culture, because the organisation is working well, senior managers are not focused on short-term fire-fighting and intervention, allowing them the time to concentrate on longer-term planning and more important issues. They are operating with timely and accurate information, which means they can make intuitive, high quality and far-reaching decisions – and that means the organisation is able to cope well with change.

It is worth saying at this stage that you are unlikely to find entire organisations evincing the features that characterise an Imaginist culture – and that's true as I take you through the rest of the higher level cultures described in this model. It is more likely that these features will be found in parts of an organisation, sometimes just in the way key individuals operate and create the culture around them. However, as the best companies have learned, the influence of a few inspirational, Imaginist-style people can be sufficient to pull the whole organisation up the management evolutionary spiral.

Bringing such people into an organisation at this stage can be an important catalyst for innovation, growth and improvement. But it won't work if the foundations aren't sound – introducing an Imaginist manager into an organisational culture that has not evolved to the appropriate level will be frustrating for them and counterproductive for the organisation.

I saw a good example of a shift from Pragmatic/Aligned through Empiricist to Imaginist in a small software company that was predominantly Pragmatic/Aligned in its management style, until they appointed a helpdesk manager whose qualities changed the way the organisation worked. He started to impose strict control over the way the company responded to customer calls for help and advice. Calls were graded by urgency and any failure to respond was immediately escalated to the Managing Director. The data was analysed and monitored. Over the space of just a few months the rest of the company started to become more Empiricist in its culture and the two founders of the company began to ask their customers more searching questions about the service they experienced. That led to a closer relationship with some key clients and an opportunity to extend their services into new areas. That in turn caused the two founders to take the time to work out a 3-year plan for expansion, looking further out and daring to think about markets they had not considered before. They involved their team in this planning exercise, which raised the level of trust and motivation – a typical side-effect of what was, by then, an Imaginist style of management.

A company that finds and recruits key managers who can work in an Imaginist style is probably headed up by a Systemist CEO. Let's swing the pendulum and explore what else that organisational culture means for an organisation.

Level 8: Systemist

You have seen how the individual working in a culturally mature, well-run organisation can respond by bringing Imaginist qualities to

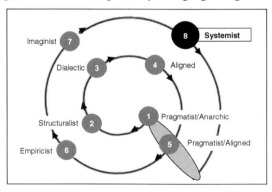

the organisation. The equivalent EXTERNAL response is the Systemist management style. This is primarily a culture brought to the organisation by its top management, usually the CEO and the Board. A Systemist manager understands that the organisation, its customers and suppliers, comprise a system and that making changes in one part of the system will affect the rest. He/she also recognises that the people in the system (including customers and suppliers) are multi-faceted and complex, operating in a social context and with needs and aspirations of their own. A systems perspective looks at the whole, over a long-term timescale so a Systemist leadership style is one where the CEO leads from the front but steers from behind, intervening to build longer-term change, rather than intervening in day-to-day operational issues.

You may have seen the TV 'troubleshooting' series in which a CEO of a UK hospital made the mistake of hiring the consultant Gerry Robinson and agreeing to be filmed while Gerry demolished his management style in public. He is now well-known for the fact that none of his hospital managers and staff knew what he looked like! He saw himself as leading from behind and was very successful in managing government targets and getting funding, but had forgotten that a leader must also be visible.

He brought Gerry in because his ideas for improving performance in the hospital were not being taken up by his team. Progress on a number of important projects had stalled. As Gerry quickly showed, the problem turned out not to lie with the team but, at root, with the disempowering effect of his absence from the table when the changes were being discussed.

To be successful the Systemist CEO makes him/herself visible and available, and is vocal in championing change, but sees his/her role in working to enable the right environment for change to occur, connecting people together, intervening only at the systems level, empowering others to take up the cause and make it happen and making the most of the creative capacities of the Imaginist managers. That enables the organisation to become a 'learning organisation'.

Leaders who try to micro-manage and don't trust their managers to make decisions may succeed in the short-term but ultimately they will fail. But those who set (and clearly communicate) the goals, step back and allow their managers to work out how to achieve them, will succeed. They will tap into a rich vein of creativity and innovation.

But note that this style only works if the organisation has a strong Imaginist culture at senior management level and an aligned workforce that needs little day-to-day, hands-on management to function smoothly.

A CEO employing a Systemist style of management can be compared to the captain of an oil supertanker who sets his 30° course change several miles ahead to give the vessel enough time to respond[9]. Transformational changes are a bit like that – the strategies and plans that trigger the changes need to be put in place and actioned well in advance of the apparent need for the change. It takes well-informed and inspired leadership and it is no accident that such leaders emerge in some of the best-run companies.

Systemist management needs the best attributes of each successive level up the spiral of management style to be in place in order to succeed.

When I started to research the management literature for examples of the Systemist management style, I discovered that most of the famous transformational corporate leaders, like Jack Welsh at GE, Steve Jobs at Apple and (perhaps less well-known but equally interesting) Carlos Ghosn at Nissan, were actually forceful characters who were adept at working at a strategic, systemic level but could not be accused of leading from behind! It seems that history doesn't recognise the Systemist leader unless he or she also has a strong enough personality to 'star' in a management textbook. However these leaders did inspire – and gave their senior managers the space and authority to take important decisions and make things happen, which a Systemist manager needs to do, so I cannot but offer them as examples.

I have only one example to offer from my own experience that illustrates some of the qualities of a Systemist management style. As

---

[9] I have to report that I used this metaphor recently and someone in the audience kindly informed me that modern oil tankers can turn far more quickly – time to find a new metaphor!

a very 'wet behind the ears' graduate entrant into BT many years ago, I was assigned to 'shadow' an older, very experienced senior manager in charge of an Area office. He had hundreds of engineers, telephonists, office workers and even cleaners under his command. One day I was summoned to take notes at a meeting that had been called by a local engineering union leader, who was clearly upset about something. He shouted and banged the table in order to get his points across and the BT manager responded just as vigorously, making my job as note-taker rather difficult! In the end the union official stormed out of the meeting – and the manager quietly turned to a colleague and said: "I thought John put his case quite well today – he's making quite good progress. I think we should consider asking him to speak at the next conference".

Startled, I quizzed him. "Oh, he said, John may be a union rep – and a bloody confrontational one, too! – but he is also one of my staff and it's my responsibility to bring him on and help him to make the best of himself." Astonishingly, (I thought at the time) he was able to wear two hats simultaneously – the belligerent boss who doesn't give way to union bullying and the coach/mentor who, quietly and behind the scenes, looks after his staff and seeks benefits for the organisation by developing their strengths.

That example sounds like I am focused back on the individual, and that's not an accident, as the key to the Systemist culture is the way a skilled leader can mould and direct the infrastructure and external capability of his organisation to get it to go where he wants it to go – applying systems thinking – without losing focus on the people – the personal touch. And the most important people for any organisation are the customers. Inherent in this culture is the strong focus on designing the organisation 'from the outside in'. I will return to this way of thinking in Chapter 10.

One more aspect of a Systemist culture – it recognises that the organisation is a system operating in the context of other systems, social, technological, economic... Find an organisation which has accepted its corporate social responsibilities, has built these into the very fabric of its objectives and 'lives' these values in everything it does – not just pays lip service to them – and you have probably found a good example of a Systemist culture.

There is one more step – and that does focus back on the INTERNAL axis. I am coming back to where I started, with the Pragmatic/Empowered culture.

Level 9: Pragmatic/Empowered

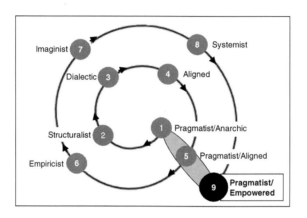

You are working in an organisation that has set itself the challenge of being the best in class. You are fully empowered to plan and manage your own workload, within a supportive Organisational Culture. This includes working collaboratively in teams and leading and participating in change projects, to continually improve the effectiveness of the organisation to meet its customers' needs. Your managers are well-informed and far-thinking, earning your trust by involving you and your team in the organisation's strategic planning and decision-making and leaving you to develop new and improved responses to the changing needs of your customers.

Sounds idyllic, doesn't it? It describes the final stage of management evolution, Pragmatic/Empowered. Do I know any organisations like this? No, although one or two came close during their best times. They are world-famous for it, of course: Innocent, Bodyshop, Ben & Jerry's... all now bought up by multinationals and doubtless working in more 'conventional' ways today. Another example I came across recently was AXA Ireland, part of the global insurance group. When the new CEO, John O'Neil, took over in 2000, the company faced heavy competition, eroding margins and a lack of customer focus which meant that the company was in real trouble. Instead of cost-cutting and re-engineering, John tapped into the creativity of his workforce to develop new insurance products and introduce far-reaching customer-focused improvements. By empowering his managers and staff, making them feel they counted, he was able to build up the business's capability and performance, so that today AXA Ireland stands at the top of the pile for customer satisfaction and profitability.

What is important about defining this ultimate organisational culture is not to compare our own work environment and despair. It is attainable and certainly aspects could be featuring in your workplace already. Empowerment is a rather maligned term. Like other aspirational descriptors (partnership, equality come to mind) it is more often claimed than realised. But I know of a customer service team whose members come together to agree their own rotas, set their own (very demanding) targets for customer satisfaction and, in the main, achieve them through determined, dedicated hard slog. They work to an annual contract that dictates the number of days in total that they need to work and the standards expected of them, but leaves it up to them to decide when they work and how they deliver these standards.

I have seen how a mail order company has succeeded in gaining fanatical customer loyalty by empowering its people to 'go the extra mile' when it comes to dealing with customers. They don't need to ask whether it's okay to send a customer flowers to say 'thank you' for some useful feedback, or to phone a supplier to pass on a compliment from a customer. If one of the senior management team is visiting the warehouse and a box needs packing, they will roll up their sleeves and give a hand. A bit disconcerting for the poor visitor who was getting a guided tour – me! – but totally empowering for the team, who used the opportunity to show the manager an idea that had come up in their quality improvement meetings.

Or what about the hotel whose staff pride themselves on knowing every customer's name within an hour of their registering – not because there is a manager behind them with a whip, but because that's who they are and that's the quality of service each of the staff stands for. Their strong sense of their own value aligned closely with that of the company they worked for.

Empowerment of the people carrying out the work is key to the capability of an organisation to embrace change and take advantage of new ways of working. Unless they are confident in their own identity in the organisation, staff won't look 'over the wall' to find out about the needs and concerns of their colleagues in other departments. And without that wider understanding, they won't accept change unless it satisfies the narrow "what's in it for me" condition.

I have drawn my examples from the service and retail sectors, as that is where the most obvious examples are, but I am sure that you can quote instances that take us into other sectors, too. These are people who have been able to take pride in their work, for whom recognition as 'excellent' is an important part of their identity. They do not exist in isolation. They would not survive in an organisational culture that did not nurture such behaviour. John Seddon, author of *Systems Thinking in the Public Sector*,[10] said it best: "Behaviour is a product of the system you put people in." (He pops up again in Chapter 10.)

So the pendulum has swung full circle and I have brought you back to the start – pragmatism rules, okay?

The evolutionary journey from Pragmatic/anarchic, through Pragmatic/aligned to Pragmatic/empowered confirms that it is not the organisation and its rules and processes or even its use of people that makes it successful.

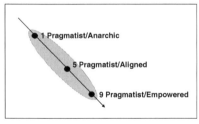

It is the people themselves, their aspirations, their dedication, their creativity. Sometimes, as we

---

[10] *Systems Thinking in the Public Sector: The Failure of the Reform Regime.... and a Manifesto for a Better Way* – John Seddon (2008)

get bogged down writing reports and delivering targets, it's worth remembering that.

Well, that is the Organisational Culture model. Nine pen pictures which can be referenced as discrete styles, but which sit on an evolutionary spiral and form a route-map towards the higher level organisational cultures we would all like to see operating in organisations we know and love (!).

If you work in a large organisation, did you recognise it? Or as a consultant or IT service provider, did you recognise your client?

The chances are you have focused on the negative aspects, such as the 'silo working' in a Structuralist culture, or the failure of your organisation to build a Dialectic culture to enable people to invent their own route-map to the future, before rationalising processes in order to improve efficiency.

Chapter 16, in the Assessment and Implementation section of the book, will show how you can use the model to navigate up the spiral, focusing on the positives at each level and developing the capability to move from an existing dominant management style that may not be serving your organisation very well any more, to a more mature and empowering culture. The chapter will also suggest what to expect if you do not make the shift.

A closer look at the EXTERNAL axis

You may have noticed that as one progresses up the organisational culture spiral, one of the characteristics of the cultures on the EXTERNAL axis is the strength of the organisation's process management.

A Structuralist culture is based on systems and rules. Its success comes from being able to move away from the ad hoc approach of the Pragmatic/Anarchic culture towards the use of routine, consistently repeatable processes. Its failure is often its inability to shift its culture away from this strongly compliant way of working – it gets bogged down by thinking about the world purely in process terms: targets, performance indicators, cost-benefit analysis, systems.

The power of the Rationalist, Aligned culture comes from the way that everyone is working consistently within systems created to achieve success.

And the ability of a CEO operating in a Systemist culture to focus on longer-term change is dependent on the organisation working efficiently.

So while the **effectiveness** of the organisation comes from its people, its ability to deliver results **efficiently** comes from how consistently and well it manages the systems and processes right across the organisation. As I looked for the barriers to change, the lack of discipline and inadequate business process capability of an organisation turned out to be an important factor in its own right. The next chapter therefore looks at business process capability – the other half of organisational capability in the INPACT triangle.

ORGANISATIONAL CAPABILITY

4

Mapping Your Organisation's Business Process Capability

The way an organisation manages its processes has a direct bearing on its ability to introduce enterprise-wide process changes. If there are no standard systems and everyone is 'doing their own thing', or if there are such systems but people are ignoring or working around them, it will clearly be more difficult to get take-up and use of new systems and processes. Much of this can be discussed using the Organisational Culture model but there is also another way to look at business process capability, which adds a different dimension to our understanding of the problem.

The model I use is one that you may have come across – Watts Humphrey's Capability Maturity Model (CMM)[11].

Watts Humphrey developed the model at the Software Engineering Institute (SEI), Carnegie Mellon University in 1986-9 to be able to assess the capability of software developers to deliver software projects to the US government. It has since been superseded for that purpose by a more sophisticated version, but the original is widely recognised as a useful generic tool and adopted by

---

[11] Watts Humphrey – *Managing the Software Process* (1989)

management consultants the world over, to understand the business process capability maturity of organisations more generally.

CMM comprises a 6-step classification system to describe processes, from Ad hoc to Integrated, and associates the capability to manage these processes, from Chaotic to Cooperative Optimisation.

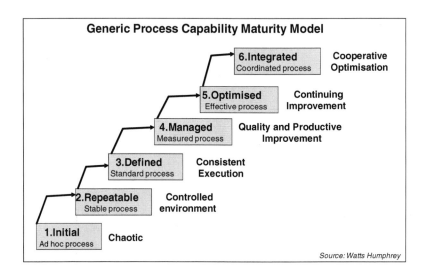

The model is concerned with the specific work that an organisation is doing to bring its processes up to an optimal level of efficiency.

The CMM model shows how the lack of even basic management controls at Level 1 leads to chaos. I saw this in a family-owned manufacturing company. Ad hoc policies and processes were invented and re-invented every time anyone encountered a new situation: a customer wanted a discount but there was no policy or system to deal with that, so one was created. But nobody else knew about it, so the next time a customer wanted a discount, a new policy and process was invented.

A complaint was handled differently every time, depending on who received it, and nobody thought to share the learning that came from resolving it. The plethora of spreadsheets, methods, rules and procedures in this CMM Level 1 organisation was mind-boggling – I counted 9 databases all with similar information on them. Not even the people working there knew about most of them!

It is obvious that the basic management controls to enable repeated use of systems and processes (CMM Level 2) were sorely lacking in that company. But just putting these in place does not mean people will adhere to them. To achieve a more consistent use of process requires strong management and a disciplined approach to compliance. These are qualities seen in organisations that are at Level 3 on the CMM ladder.

Getting beyond Level 3 requires attention to the efficiency of the process. What is the process costing? Are there more cost-effective ways to achieve the objective? Is every activity adding value? These are the questions that will need answering in order to gain Level 4 process capability. And then it is just a question of how much effort you put into improving the management and measurement of your processes. CMM Level 5, optimised process, is not a goal that most organisations need to worry about and Level 6 uses terminology that is usually bandied about but rarely achieved in 'softer' contexts, let alone the highly empirical one of systems and process design and operation: coordinated, co-operative, integrated...

As with the Organisational Culture model, I have adopted elements of the CMM classification approach that offer a practical and relatively easy way to spot where an organisation lies on the business process capability ladder. I have not adhered to the CMM methodologies that the model spawned, however the 6-step model itself suggests the kind of questions that you could be asking to assess your organisation's business process capability. It also provides a route-map for improvement.

For example, try identifying the sentence, from the set below, that most closely describes the business process capability in your part of the organisation.

- Almost all of the information I need regularly from other parts of the organisation is readily available from our systems and can be relied upon to be accurate (CMM Level 2 or above)

- Our processes are clearly understood and complied with and we use standard systems and processes wherever possible across the organisation (CMM Level 3 or above)

- We measure our performance against targets and strive to continuously improve our processes (CMM Level 4 or above)

The majority of larger organisations will have some standardised processes, which would suggest a capability at Level 3 (consistent execution of standard process), but in fact many struggle to manage these systems and have aspects of their operation that lack basic management control, so are only at Level 1 (chaotic use of ad hoc processes).

Those that have long experience of working with sophisticated enterprise-wide systems may be operating predominantly at Level 4 (managed & measured process), perhaps with some processes at Level 5 (optimised), perhaps even Level 6 (integrated) – although it is rare for the organisation as a whole to have reached Level 6 – that requires very sophisticated business process capability that is usually only applied to high-risk, high-value processes.

Let's look back at some of the examples quoted in earlier chapters – you will see how the CMM model offers insights into the root of some of the problems the organisations faced.

The Local Authority in Chapter 2 which tried to introduce e-procurement was not just battling against a 'silo working' culture. It didn't have the management controls in place to achieve consistency in the way its processes were carried out. If the council had been operating a standardised manual procurement process consistently across the organisation, the transition to the new portal would have been relatively easy.

The software company in Chapter 3 that moved from Pragmatic/Aligned to a more Empiricist culture when the helpdesk manager imposed new controls, also raised their business process capability due to his efforts. Where people had developed systems and processes in a fairly ad hoc way to deal with situations as they arose, the new approach was to define and rationalise these systems and processes so that data was held once only in the company. That contributed significantly to the ability of the two founders to understand their business, as they were able to access accurate and up-to-date information when they needed it, instead of having to go and ask someone to produce it each time. Top-performing companies have all developed sophisticated ways to benchmark their performance against their rivals.

You can see evidence of well-managed process in other examples, too. The hotel staff in the example in Chapter 3 who know every customer's name within an hour of their registering are totally dependent on their computer system giving them the information they need, when they need it – and in turn, they know how important it is to feed back accurate and timely data so their colleagues can operate at the same high levels of service quality. That discipline is a critical part of their organisational capability.

If I mapped the business process capability of the NHS Trust in Chapter 4 where silo working and tribalism are blocking all attempts to bring in new standardised systems, it would show some Level 3 capability (defined, standard process) within the walls of the clinical wards and operating theatres where patient safety was paramount, but away from these processes, the predominant capability would be at CMM Level 1 (ad hoc process) or Level 2 capability (controlled environment, repeatable process).

But it's not all routine process

One important additional consideration in assessing business process capability is the extent to which your organisation's work is routine, using repeatable processes; and to what extent it is dealing with ad hoc requirements, which need unique responses.

An example would be a civil service department where very little of their work is routine. They are there to respond to their Minister's day-to-day need for briefings, to answer questions and requests from press and public, to come up with policy and position papers and to liaise with other departments. The routine aspects are limited to data collection and reporting for cyclical and similarly predictable requirements for information. In this organisation, performance improvement needs to focus on knowledge sharing and access to expertise rather than streamlining and automating workflow. I deal with non-routine work again in Chapter 10 as part of the Delivering Successful Projects section.

By contrast, a local authority will have a multitude of services being delivered using routine processes. These may have been evolved locally and are capable of being made more efficient and effective by introducing new systems and redesigning the processes, benchmarked against good practice models across the UK.

Use the Capability Maturity Model to assess your organisation's predominant business process capability, then see how this maps on to your organisation's culture.

5

Combining the Capability Models: The Organisational Capability Indicator

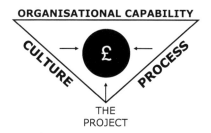

As you have no doubt worked out for yourself, the majority of organisations that are at Levels 1 and 2 on the Organisational Culture model are often also at Levels 1 or 2 on the Capability Maturity Model. Those that have moved up the organisational culture spiral to Dialectic and Aligned styles are also likely to have developed more defined and standardised systems and processes.

This is not always the case – it will depend on the nature of the organisation, the sector, the regulatory environment within which it operates and the ratio of routine to ad hoc work (as discussed earlier). An organisation with a lot of ad hoc work, like the civil service example, may have evolved to a higher level on the organisational culture spiral, without having felt the need to make the effort to raise their business process capability. The diagram shown overleaf overlays the culture and business process capability models to illustrate the relationship.

How the Capability Maturity Model relates to the Organisational Culture model

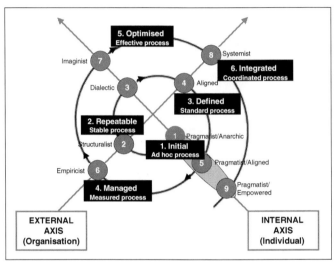

By contrast, a highly structured and regulated organisation, such as a financial services company, may have sophisticated systems and standardised processes being managed at level 3 or 4, but remain at level 1 or 2 on the organisational culture spiral. However, organisations with a lower level organisational culture are rarely capable of managing sophisticated systems and processes.

For example:

A service organisation rationalised its customer call handling by implementing a Customer Relationship Management (CRM) system – a one-stop shop where all calls were dealt with by relatively unskilled, low-cost staff. The system equipped the staff with the basic information about the services and a standard set of online forms to capture the customer requests and complaints.

This team was targeted with answering calls within a maximum number of seconds. The information was then passed back to the relevant service departments which processed the requests and dealt with the complaints. They were targeted on the number of files they processed every day.

The processes seemed to be working well. Targets were met. But customers were not happy. Why? The CRM team was more interested in meeting their performance targets than helping a customer and the service teams found that they could hit their targets by dealing with the simpler cases first... The balance between process and culture was wrong – whereas customers wanted to talk to someone who could help them, the organisation's attention was focused inwards on meeting departmental performance targets. They may have been operating a CRM system at quite a high level of business process capability (CMM Level 4 – Measured process), but the culture was predominantly Structuralist. The organisation was not capable of empowering its staff to use the CRM system properly to assist their customers.

Combining the models

Combining the two models provides a useful baseline for an organisation to assess its capability to manage change and how successful it will be in introducing cross-department systems and processes.

Combining the two models also provides us with the underlying philosophy for the INPACT approach.

Remember it from the introduction?

"An integrated and balanced focus on people and process throughout a change or transformation project is essential for success."

It can be useful to bring the process and culture capabilities together in a simple indicator graph to indicate organisational capability, as illustrated overleaf:

73

ORGANISATIONAL CAPABILITY

Organisational Culture	Business Process Capability				
	Level 1	2	3	4	5
1. Pragmatic/ Anarchic	Low	Low			
2. Structuralist	Low	Low	Med		
3. Dialectic	Low	Med	Med	Med	
4. Aligned	Med	Med	Med	High	High
5. Pragmatic/ Aligned			High	High	High
6. Empiricist			High	High	High
7. Imaginist			High	High	V.High
8. Systemist			High	V.High	V.High
9. Pragmatic/Empowered			V.High	V.High	V.High

The illustration shows how an organisation with a level 4 (Aligned) organisational culture and CMM Level 3 (Defined) process capability has a **Medium** organisational capability. That is, its capability to manage change is Medium, whereas an organisation with an organisational culture predominantly at Level 2 (Structuralist) is likely to have a CMM Level 1 or 2 process capability and a Low capability for change.

This is only meant as an illustration – obviously, each assessment will throw up different combinations and you need to pull together a much more detailed analysis than this crude indicator to use when working out what to do about the barriers to success that you have identified.

I have found, however, that a simplified 'traffic light' indicator highlighting High/Medium/Low risk serves very well to highlight capability gaps to a senior management audience – better than a more detailed analysis in some cases, if what you are seeking to do is to capture their attention.

The strong links between the 'people' and 'process' capabilities can be seen if I re-run some of the earlier examples I quoted:

Looking back to the Local Authority example, you can see how the silo culture extended to the inability of the organisation to introduce standardised systems and processes – and get them used. Senior management were less interested in improving the quality and performance of the organisation's systems and processes than in achieving their own departments' targets. The lack of mandate from the top aggravated the already poor standard of compliance and nobody except the IT Director cared about bringing in standard ways of working. This meant that the organisation was operating at a low level of efficiency and was ill-equipped to accommodate change.

Most local councils that I have worked with are at this low level of business process capability. Those few councils that have managed the transition to Level 3 (consistent use of defined process) have done so because of a more mature organisational culture. They tend to be smaller and have a strong, respected CEO, who has achieved greater cross-organisation knowledge sharing and higher levels of trust among his team, and a very good IT Director who has the authority to mandate compliance to standards. Strong leadership is a clear prerequisite for success and gaining the required levels of trust is easier in a smaller organisation.

UK public sector IT spending currently stands at £16.8bn and is set to grow to £20.2bn by 2011/12. Research suggests that less than a third of this will succeed in producing the desired performance improvements and cost savings. Would it be foolish to suggest an organisational capability survey to identify the culture and business process capability barriers and start to deal with them? This could be incorporated into government's existing Gateway Review process and might improve the levels of success.

I have focused rather a lot on understanding the two key elements of organisational capability. I don't apologise for that, as it's the foundation for the INPACT approach and the bedrock upon which a good project has to sit, but I now propose to shift the focus from assessing the organisation's overall capability to looking at specific projects and considering aspects of the planning and delivery of transformation.

In doing so, I will still be swinging the pendulum and attempting to achieve a balance between people and process. I'll start by looking at one of the most frequently cited reasons for projects to have failed: the failure of planners to gain shared perceptions of what the project will achieve and who is responsible for realising the benefits.

SECTION 2: THE PROJECT

6

Clarity of Objectives

ORGANISATIONAL CAPABILITY

£

Culture → ← Process

THE
PROJECT

I had the opportunity to work with a Business School MBA course last summer to research potential causes of project failure. In one exercise we approached project managers who were responsible for planning and implementing change projects in a number of companies. We asked them a series of questions based on the INPACT approach and then asked the same questions of a number of stakeholders in their projects.

We were quickly able to identify real disparities between what project managers were telling us about their projects and what other stakeholders thought about them. In one case, the project manager told us that all the stakeholders had been fully consulted, so he was confident that the project would succeed – but that was not the story we got from the stakeholders who responded to our questionnaire. (If I add that the organisation's culture was predominantly Structuralist and the business process capability was mostly at Level 1 (ad hoc), that probably tells you how likely they are to succeed in implementing the change.)

This research confirmed something that everyone knows, but they still don't seem to be able to achieve: getting stakeholders to agree on the objectives of a project is critical to its success.

In order to include this in the INPACT assessment, I get the statement of objectives from the project sponsor – it's usually in a project initiation or business case document. I then ask the key stakeholders three linked questions:

- In your view, what are the main objectives and benefits of the project?
- Who is responsible for delivering the benefits?
- What are your responsibilities in the project?

The greater the disparity between the stakeholder responses and that provided by the project sponsor, the less likely it is that the project will succeed. Furthermore, the vaguer the responses to the second and third questions, the more resistance you will find in rolling out the changes. It is possible to express this in a simple model.

For example, if there are 6 stakeholders and each question was worth a score of 1, the maximum score (18) would be achieved if they all had a clear understanding of the objectives which aligned with that of the project sponsor, could each identify the key people in the organisation responsible for making the changes happen once the systems were in place and could describe their own role in benefits realisation terms. (The last two are so crucial to success that I will be returning to them later in the book.)

Stakeholders	Question 1	Question 2	Question 3
	Good match = 1 Poor match = 0	If clear = 1 If vague = 0	If clear = 1 If vague = 0
1	1	1	1
2	0	0	0
3	1	1	1
4	0	0	0
5	1	1	0
6	1	0	0
TOTAL	**4**	**3**	**2**

In this example, only two of the stakeholders were clear on all three questions and the overall score was 9, i.e. 50%.

If the response you get from your stakeholders reveals more than a 25% disparity, you can expect problems. A 50% score means that if an initial communication exercise had been undertaken to gain agreement and ownership among stakeholders, it was not done well enough; or that people and situations have changed since then, so the project no longer has the priority and clarity of objectives it needs.

In some cases such consultation is undertaken so superficially ('tick the box') that there is no real recognition of the implications for the local management and workforce and no ownership of the changes they need to put in place – that should emerge during this exercise.

Disparity well above 50% probably means there has been no communication and you have a potential disaster on your hands! The worse the measure, the greater the ammunition you have to demonstrate the importance of remedial action to ensure a proper communications exercise to get people on board.

The problems that arose from the merger between the small, fast-growing company and the larger organisation that I quoted in Chapter 3, illustrate this situation very well. The cultures and capabilities of the two organisations were clearly incompatible and work was urgently needed to avoid disaster. A key finding was that the senior management in each company had very different perceptions of what the merger meant for them and their company – and any work that had been done to achieve shared objectives had been unsuccessful. So the first step was to gain clarity of objectives for the new combined organisation. I started by addressing what the customers wanted and ensuring that this intelligence was widely shared and acted upon. Only then could the new company move forward successfully.

It is important not just to establish that stakeholders have a shared understanding of the project objectives but also to check that their roles in implementing the project are clearly defined. A colleague, Mark Connell, puts it very well: "I have frequently worked on projects where stakeholders think that they are there merely to take the results of the project or shout at the project team when that does not happen."

Stakeholders need to recognise that it is their role to raise issues and concerns, lobby for project resources, make change requests and keep the project manager focused on the business benefits.

Helping stakeholders understand their role at an early stage will give the project a better chance of succeeding. This includes the stakeholder being accountable for implementing the changes needed locally to ensure performance-related benefits are realised. I will return to this in Chapter 14 when I look at the way a Benefits Realisation Plan can change the dynamics of a project.

One approach which has been proven to help in gaining stakeholder clarity of objectives and commitment to playing their part, is to create a Stakeholder Map, which sets out these aspects in some detail and also enables you to check, record and report back their input to the project sponsor.

If the objectives of the project are reasonably clear, the next question is whether the project as a whole lies within the capability of the organisation. That's where the Exponential Complexity tool comes into play...

7

The Exponential Complexity Tool

ORGANISATIONAL CAPABILITY

Culture → £ ← Process

THE PROJECT

Every day we read about high profile IT projects that fail or are going to cost many times what was expected, are years late and do not deliver the expected benefits. I seem to have spent a substantial part of my career looking at why this is and trying to overcome the obstacles to success.

There are obviously many of these, from poor articulation of requirements, through inadequate resourcing, lack of experience and insufficient 'clout' of project managers, right down to lack of end-user training and support, but when I was developing INPACT, what I needed was a simple, single measure to assess and express the chances of these kinds of projects succeeding or falling short. And I realised that COMPLEXITY was the common factor.

It didn't seem to matter how well a project was planned – if it was too complex, it would fail, or only deliver too little, too late and over budget. And a strange thing – it was always going fine...until suddenly it wasn't! The speed with which projects fail can be breathtaking. Here's an example:

In 2004, HM Prison Service commissioned a new system, C-NOMIS, to give prison and probation officers real-time access to offenders' records. In June 2005 the approved lifetime cost of the project was quoted as £234m.

In March 2007, the Home Secretary is quoted as saying: "the main C-NOMIS base release, encompassing full prison and probation functionality, will be available no later than July 2008" but in July we heard that C-NOMIS is two years behind schedule! The estimated lifetime project costs had trebled to £690m and the Ministry of Justice decided to suspend the project.

The Commons Public Accounts Committee reported on that project was a catalogue of mistakes (they judged it: "a spectacular failure – in a class of its own"!) but one thing shone through: insufficient resources and structures had been put in place to deliver such a complex project.

It wasn't just that the project was big and ambitious. It was more that the mechanisms for coping with the complexity were not adequate – it got away from them. And this was a cumulative process.

Let's look at a private sector example:

In 2004, HP's project managers knew all of the things that could go wrong with their ERP centralisation programme. But they just didn't plan for so many of them to happen at once. The project eventually cost HP $160 million in order backlogs and lost revenue—more than five times the project's estimated cost.

Gilles Bouchard, then CIO of HP's global operations is quoted as saying: "We had a series of small problems, none of which individually would have been too much to handle. But together they created the perfect storm."

So it is quite often a series of smaller problems that add up to a significant failure.

The recent collapse of Terminal 5's baggage handling system on the terminal's opening day in April 2008 provides a useful illustration of that principle. That resulted in over 28,000 lost bags, 700 cancelled planes and more than 150,000 disrupted passengers.

The press had a field day: "The Terminal 5 debacle is a national disgrace" (*Daily Mail*, 14 April 2008). But what had gone wrong?

The first problem was a lack of staff car parking spaces, so when the baggage handlers arrived, they couldn't park. By now the first planes were landing. Then there was only one employee security checkpoint operating, creating a further bottleneck for staff.

When they did get into the terminal, some staff found they were unable to log on to the computer system and another automated handheld system was telling handlers to put bags onto flights that had already left, leaving bags piling up unattended elsewhere. The first flights had now left without bags, creating the first backlog.

The problems were now compounded by a design decision to house the managers in a control centre in another part of the terminal, so they could supervise and communicate electronically. That meant there were no managers on the ground to re-allocate work and sort things out.

The pile-up of bags now meant that there was a shortage of bar-reading storage bins that routed bags to the right planes. By 4pm, with too many bags, too few storage bins, an already clogged conveyor belt system and handling staff under severe pressure, all it took was a fresh wave of new luggage to choke the system to a standstill. The conveyor belt taking the bags ground to a halt and minutes later BA was forced to suspend all baggage check-in.

Looking at these examples, I realised that there was a pattern. Why was it that these projects were always going fine, until they weren't? Why did it just take one or two small additional factors to create a runaway disaster? And then the penny dropped. Project complexity is exponential.

"The greatest shortcoming of the human race is our inability to understand the exponential function." (Professor Albert Bartlett, emeritus Professor of Physics at the University of Colorado at Boulder.)

We live in a world that can change exponentially – but we have brains that are hardwired to plot things out linearly – the software in our brains compels us to think about progressions as being simple arithmetic ones. So, despite being surrounded by exponential change (population explosion, energy depletion, cumulative growth of capital etc), and intellectually understanding it, we seem constantly to underestimate exponential scales.

Now I began to understand why these project disasters keep on happening – and to experienced managers who should have known

85

better. They were in denial about how complex their projects were.

So I looked for the factors behind project complexity – factors that could be easily quantified and that, together, would give us a good predictor of project success or failure. I needed a minimum of three factors in order to develop an exponential model to represent project complexity – more may reflect reality but that would make the model more difficult to use. These factors needed to be easy to identify and quantify, representative of the causes of risk in complex projects and robust enough that they gave an accurate predictor of complexity.

After some experimentation, I found that the complexity of projects depends largely on the combination of these three factors:

1. The number of people or **S**takeholders involved
2. The number of business activities or **P**rocesses affected
3. Elapsed **T**ime (in months) to implement

If you are planning to implement an IT-based change or transformation project and can't currently provide good estimates for each of these, make sure they are on your list of issues to address before you go any further.

Number of people or Stakeholders involved:
More people = more complex = higher risk

The more people (roles) are involved in the decision-making and implementation of the project e.g. IT manager, user groups, product suppliers, consultants and sub-contractors, the more difficult it is to make sure you have consulted and trained all who need to be involved.

Number of business activities or Processes affected:
More ambitious = more complex = higher risk

The more far-reaching the solution, in terms of the business activities affected, the harder it is to make sure you have covered all the links and interfaces with other activities. Implementation is also more complicated and you cannot afford for the business to come to a stop because the new system doesn't work properly. Good practice is to break large-scale requirements down into smaller projects and always make sure you have contingency plans in place – you can't afford to stop your business.

Elapsed Time to implement:
Longer to implement = more complex = higher risk

The longer it takes from your initial definition of what you want to achieve, to the time you can actually get the system to deliver these benefits, the more likely it is your project will fail. This is because the world does not stand still. Your needs change and you will be tempted to add new requirements and that adds complexity.

Good practice is to avoid lengthy project cycles (for example, 3 months is a long time for a software development project) and always control change requests rigorously – or suffer the fate of the London Ambulance Service and countless other examples where system implementations became top-heavy and never made it.

The Exponential Complexity Tool

Put these three factors into an equation: $S \times P \times T$ and you have the Exponential Complexity Tool.

When I get to this point in the workshops I run, I ask delegates to first tell me where they thought their project sits on the scale:

Simple / Not simple / Complex / Too complex

Then they try the equation out for themselves – and I hand out calculators. People look surprised – "I can do this in my head", they say, until they try. Try it for yourself. With a specific project in mind, put a number in each of the right-hand boxes.

S: the number of stakeholders involved (an approximation might be everyone represented on steering and project groups)	S =
P: the number of business activities and processes that will be affected (for example the number of manual processes an automation project will 'touch' and change):	P =
T: Expected implementation timescale in months (from issue of spec/ITT to planned completion of roll-out)	T =

Don't worry about getting all the numbers absolutely right – an approximation will do for the purpose of the exercise. People do get stressed about estimating two of the factors, in particular:

- Stakeholders – this might be everyone represented on the project's steering group or project board. In some cases you might need to extend this group, particularly if you are aware that the consultation process didn't include all those affected by the changes.

- Timescale – typically from the issue of a specification and Invitation to Tender (so the business case has already been approved) to the completion of roll-out. But in some cases you may need to modify that to suit your own situation.

Now multiply **S** x **P** x **T**.

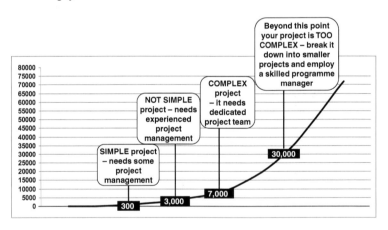

Plot the result on the Exponential Complexity Model chart below. Where does this actually put your project on the Complexity scale?

Arrived at a number? Here's a quick guide to what it means:

Simple project – if the total scores around 300 or less, yours is a relatively simple project. Follow a structured project plan and get help if you have not tackled this type of project before.

Not simple – if the number is between 300 and 3,000, make sure you have planned the project properly and brought in an experienced project manager – it isn't as simple as you thought. And don't let it grow like Topsy!

Complex project – a figure between 3,000 and 7,000 shows that yours is actually a complex project. Appoint a sponsor who will champion the project, select a project team with sufficient experience and identify a business manager who will keep the project focused on getting the business benefits you first defined. Whichever project management method you use, stick to it! Make sure senior management is being kept in the picture and that there is an option to stop the project if it isn't going to plan. If you don't have the experience to do this yourselves, scale down the project or seek help – *before* you start.

Too complex: a figure between 7,000 and 30,000 is definitely getting too complex to be dealt with as a single project and beyond 30,000 you definitely need to break it down into separate projects and employ a skilled programme management team. Highly complex projects like this require full-time, very experienced programme managers and dedicated implementation resources. Failure to allocate sufficient skills and resources will result in the new systems not being taken up within the planned timescale – leading, at best, to lower than planned efficiency benefits, and too frequently, to total disaster.

Most people who undertake this exercise thought their project was quite a lot simpler than it shows up to be on the complexity scale. And that is really the learning point the tool is intended to get across.

Like the Change Equation, the secret is the ' x ' or 'times' operand which means that unless all three numbers you have input to the model are very small, you are soon dealing with a Complexity Factor in thousands.

The exponential nature of complexity gets away from people when they are planning projects, but it is probably the most important information you need to plan a successful project.

89

What are the implications of exponential complexity?

Let's look at a typical corporate transformation project.

The objective in this example was to improve the way the organisation manages its procurement. The project was intended to implement a standardised set of online procurement processes, based around an e-procurement system linked to the finance system, that would enable the whole organisation to requisition, authorise, order, receive invoices and pay for goods and services in a properly managed and controlled fashion, with substantial cost and efficiency savings.

Because procurement is carried out all over the organisation and the new system would enable self-service ordering and authorisation online, this project was expected to directly affect people across the 7 departments in the organisation. These are represented on the project steering group by 15 people but it was clear that quite a few other stakeholders were not represented, including key suppliers who had to modify their interface with their customer, so a more accurate number might be 30.

The online system was planned to completely or partly replace around 20 existing manual procedures and have an impact on a further 10.

It was planned to take 12 months to roll out the new e-procurement system, load the content, train the users and start getting the benefits, which would then take a further 6 months to build up to a positive Return on Investment (ROI).

The complexity factor can be calculated as: 30 x 30 x 12 (ignoring the savings build-up period) = 10,800.

That places the project, which this organisation considers a relatively low-profile IT infrastructure change, well beyond the Complex point on the Exponential Complexity scale and high enough that the warning bells should start to ring.

Note that recovering from a project that became too complex and failed is not simply a matter of reverting to 'business as usual'. Often severe damage has been done: to morale, to performance and to the bottom line. Just as we underestimate complexity, it is easy to understate the cost of a failed project.

Complexity in context

Obviously, it is too simplistic to consider project complexity in isolation. The relative relationship between project complexity and organisational capability also needs to be considered. If an organisation has the maturity and experience to cope with significant change and has the process capability to improve its systems and processes in a disciplined fashion, a complex project should be within its grasp.

However, more complex projects are unlikely to be fully successful in an immature organisation i.e. level 1 or 2 organisational culture and anything lower than level 3 process capability.

If you have been applying the models as you have been reading through this book, you can gauge this for yourself by taking the combined organisational capability value you arrived at in Chapter 3 (High/Medium/Low) and plotting it against the complexity value (Simple/Not Simple/ Complex/Too Complex) as the two axes of a simple chart, illustrated here.

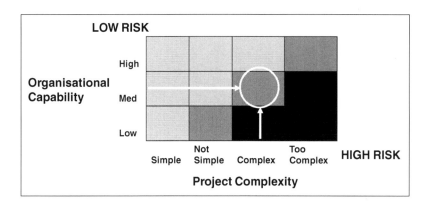

So what does this tell us? In simple terms, whether your project is high-risk, medium-risk or low-risk. In the illustration, the project is Complex and the organisation has a Medium Capability, so the indicator shows Medium Risk.

As with the capability 'traffic light' indicator, this is far too high-level to tell you in any detail what to do about the gaps – that has to come from your underlying analysis – but clearly, a high or medium risk project should be reconsidered. That might mean lowering the ambitions of the project. It almost certainly will mean undertaking work to improve the capability of the organisation, before embarking on the project. It is also likely that the skills and resources allocated to the project will not be sufficient.

A review of the Project Resource Plan may show that a more experienced project or programme manager needs to be brought in. It may also be that more department resources need to be committed to local implementation.

The financial services company that acquired and merged with its rival, quoted in Chapter 3, had left the physical movement of departments to the estates manager in the parent company, who wisely identified that this move was highly complex and also recognised that the company had under-resourced the rest of the merger, including the changes to systems and processes. When we discussed this, he calculated the complexity of the 6 months project as over 3,000, so past the Not Simple point, but the planning had been done as if the project was just 'Simple – needs some project management'. If he hadn't stepped in and managed the whole inter-dependent process of planning the office and systems move more carefully, the merger would have stalled altogether.

This chapter focused on the exponential nature of complexity and our apparent inability to deal with it. In the case of the Prison Service's C-Nomis programme, mentioned earlier, the National Audit Office found that: "in 2005 alone there were an estimated 300-400 requests for changes to the original requirements". This unmanaged rise in the level of complexity is clearly unsustainable and was a principal factor in the project's spiralling costs and eventual failure.

The same happened with the London Ambulance Service so many years ago. It seems we never learn... The government has introduced Gateway Reviews into all its IT-based change projects, in the hope of preventing any more fiascos – but this only does part of the job. The risk assessment questionnaire does identify size and scope of the project as risk factors, but it ignores the risks involved in longer implementation timescales. It considers the potential impact of the change on the organisation, partners and customers/citizens and checks that the project is fully resourced, but amazingly does not ask about the extent that those resources are allocated to change management. It also entirely fails to address the organisational cultural or process capability readiness for change which represent the real cause of a lot of the lack of success in public sector projects. The focus is more on the project as a technology delivery project which, as we all very well know, is the worst thing you can do!

I will return to these issues in Chapter 17, 'Overcoming the Barriers to Success: the Action Plan'. Meanwhile, I want to move on to look at a number of other key elements which I have identified as contributing to a project's success or failure and which need to be incorporated into any assessment. These include the drivers for change, process visibility, distrust, resistance to new technology and benefits realisation. Quite a mixed bag! I have grouped them under the section heading: Delivering Successful Projects.

SECTION 3: DELIVERING SUCCESSFUL PROJECTS

8

The Drivers for Change and How to Harness Them

I was running a software quality workshop a few years back for a group of 25 software project managers. I asked them: "When a new system is implemented to improve efficiency, who is responsible for actually achieving the benefits?"

"I am" said one project manager. "Really?" I said.

"Oh, I see – it's the software supplier" came the response.

"Really?" I said, again.

After a pause for thought: "You mean it's the client"

"Okay – but who?"

Tentatively: "The department manager?"

Silence, from me…

"The system users?"

No doubt you are way ahead of me… But this is a serious point. Unless the people actually using the new system or improved process are involved in planning and implementing the changes to what they do, the project will not realise the anticipated benefits. As the comedian George Carlin famously put it: "I put a dollar in one of those change machines. Nothing changed."

It's people, not systems and processes that are the drivers for change. We all know this, so why is it so hard for us to put this understanding into practice?

Sometimes it is the culture of the organisation that works against gaining involvement and commitment at the local level, as the London Council and NHS examples illustrated. Often the 'technology push' mentality still prevails – it's the IT department's responsibility to manage IT projects. Maybe the management board or the politicians have set the deadlines and they are unrealistic, so they haven't allocated enough budget, time and skilled resources to ensuring that people are fully bought in. But unless people are fully bought in, of course, nothing will get done.

The Change Equation

One of the best ways to articulate this – and a useful tool when trying to get change to happen – is the Change Equation. Originally developed by David Gleicher in the '60s[12], this has been adopted and adapted by consultants under many names and in many guises over the years.

I found this a really useful tool over the years; extrapolating from the concepts underlying the equation has led me to the INPACT approach and this book – hence the title. My version has evolved in use and differs in emphasis slightly from the original.

---

[12] Beckhard, R. and David Gleicher – *Organization Development: Strategies and Models* (1969)

Why do we need an equation? Well, change is difficult and scary. It's expensive and distracting. It takes us out of our comfort zone and demands that we confront our fears ('Do I have the skills?' 'Will I screw up?' Will I have a job afterwards?'). This fear creates inertia, or worse – it can push people in the opposite direction, fleeing and hiding from the need to change.

Fear and aversion to change are built into the way we think and this way of thinking is often the main reason that organisations find it so hard to generate the momentum for change. No wonder, then, that making change happen is often illustrated like this:

Let's call all this the Cost of Change and put it on the right hand side of the equation:

… > **Cost of Change**

If the cost of change is so great, what do we need to do to create the momentum to overcome it? Well, the first element is **Vision**.

The drivers for change: 1. Vision

Any project needs a shared vision to ensure everyone is moving in the same, new, direction. What's the vision for your project? It may be:

- Delivery of better quality services to customers
- Cost and efficiency savings

Or more high-level:

- Restructuring and refocusing of your organisation to meet changing market conditions

This vision is not the starting point – it will have emerged from the analysis of the problem being tackled. In most transformation projects, that analysis will have included carrying out a top-down diagnosis, followed by consultation and brainstorming to arrive at something tangible, coherent and *shared.*

The purpose of the shared vision is to provide the reference framework for the transformational process – the basis on which people can move forward together.

So our Change Equation now has 2 components:

Vision > Change

Is having a Vision sufficient to overcome the fear and inertia of change? Maybe not...

How often have you been carried away with enthusiasm by a good presenter, setting out their vision, then found the enthusiasm dissipates little by little as you get back to your day-to-day problems? So having a vision on its own is not enough to drive change.

One of the reasons for this – and a primary cause for change projects to deliver poor results – is that the vision (the project's objectives) is often not sufficiently clearly understood by all the stakeholders – it is not really SHARED.

One of our INPACT assessment exercises puts this question to a group of project stakeholders: "What is this project for, what will it achieve and who is responsible for making it happen?" (Notice that last part!). I rarely get the same answer from any of the stakeholders.

They may have agreed to the project following an excellent presentation by the sponsor and they may have ticked the box as part of a formal consultation exercise, but in practice giving a presentation and carrying out a formal consultation often gains no more than a superficial acceptance, without the real commitment required to get the change implemented.

That takes time and resources which, when it comes to the crunch, managers and staff will claim not to have.

The degree to which stakeholder perceptions differ, provides a good predictor of the problems that will occur when implementing the changes. Just carrying out the exercise can often remedy this to some degree, unless it is symptomatic of a more deep-seated communication problem which the Organisational Culture model will have already suggested. But even where the vision has been successfully communicated, it seems that it is not enough on its own to drive change. Why? Because it does not place sufficient focus on the practical steps that need to be taken to implement the change.

The drivers for change: 2. First steps

To drive change, we need to have the first steps clearly set out. These might be in the form of a route-map or project plan that people can understand and use to develop their own plans for the action they need to take.

Only at this level of practicality can we engage people and gain some degree of commitment.

So the equation now says:

Vision + First steps > Cost of Change

Is that enough?

The research carried out when the model was first developed suggested that even when the first steps were clearly set out and everyone knew what they had to do, change still didn't happen.

What's missing? It's the energy and momentum for change.

And where does this have to come from? The project champion? The project manager? No... it has to come from the people who need to make the changes – the system and process users.

Consider an example: a group of managers agree to take action to make something happen, so they go away with a clear understanding of what needs to be done, but at the next meeting it appears that little progress has been made. Why?

Everyone has been too busy, other things came up, it turned out to be more complicated that they had thought... The energy that was needed to drive this project was missing – it had failed to build up any momentum, despite the clarity of vision and agreed objectives.

What went wrong? In my experience, two factors are at work: lack of accountability and lack of motivation. Making people personally accountable for results is key to getting things done and must be part of any good project management, but it's still not enough – people have to be motivated to give the project priority and devote the extra time and effort – the ENERGY – that it will require.

And that motivation doesn't seem to be generated simply by people being given a vision and a route-map. Here's why:

Think back to when you made an important personal change, like giving up smoking. Did you make the change because people around you suggested you should? Did you do it because TV programmes and magazines told you to? If so, did the change succeed? Or did you go back to your old ways?

I am quite sure that if you made the change and stuck to it, you actually did so because *you* had decided that you wanted to make the change – it was *you* that told you to do it, not anyone else. So the motivation – and the energy to change – comes from the person making the change.

How *do* you tap into this energy? By getting THEM to tell YOU why things have to change...

The drivers for change: 3. Dissatisfaction

It's only when people have convinced themselves that things are NOT okay and that there is a need to do something about it NOW, that new ways of thinking can be introduced. Then you can tap into the energy that's needed to overcome the resistance and inertia. John

Kotter, in his book *Heart of Change*[13], calls this 'Raising the sense of urgency'.

Unless people can tell you why things have to change, they won't. But how do you accomplish this?

What you are trying to do is to trigger a reaction that shifts people out of their complacency. "Well, maybe things are not okay, and we do have to do something about it, but..." "Actually, we all know we need to make the change, it's just that..." You need to get them to the stage where the status quo is no longer acceptable TO THEM.

You will find that many of the tools covered in this book, used as the circumstances dictate, can achieve this mindset shift. For example, just getting people to identify where they are on the organisational culture spiral can get them motivated. Involving them in redesigning processes has a similar effect, gaining their ownership of the changes.

A good approach to focus people on this issue and get them to think about it, is the use of the 'Incisive Questions' technique:

"Do your projects come in on time and achieve their objectives in full?"
"Most of them."

"What percentage don't?"
"Oh, probably 10-20%."

"How much does this mean you are losing in cost benefits every year?"
"I don't know – maybe £xxxk"

"Really?" (showing your surprise should make your victim a bit less complacent about this loss) *"Are you happy about that?"*
"Well no, I suppose not."

Notice how each question asks for more detail, driving the respondent to think deeper about his own statement. When they have

---

[13] John P Kotter and Dan S Cohen – *The Heart of Change: Real-Life Stories of How People Change Their Organizations* (2002)

expressed dissatisfaction with the situation they are in, you can come in with the new idea:

> *"Would it be useful if we worked out you how you can cut this waste in half so you could use the resources to deliver more projects and increase profit?"*
>
> *"Er, yes – how do we do that?"*

Notice that the idea was phrased so that 'we' would work together and 'you' could make the improvement.

The final *'yes, how do we do that?'* is the signal that you have triggered the necessary dissatisfaction and have their permission to start tapping into the energy for change.

So now the equation looks like this:

Vision + First steps + Dissatisfaction > Cost of Change

Except that I need to do one more thing. The '+' sign suggests that you could take any element out and the equation will stand. You have seen that's not the case – all three elements on the left hand side of the equation are essential to overcome the inertia and enable change to happen. So I need to change the operands to 'x':

Vision x First steps x Dissatisfaction > Cost of Change

I have used approaches based on this equation in most of my facilitation and change management work over the years to gain the commitment and energy of the people who have to actually deliver the benefits of the transformation project.

In the next chapter I want to take another, slightly different approach to the challenge of gaining commitment. Don't be put off by the chapter heading: Process Visibility – you'll see where I am going with this.

9

Process Visibility

Mapping and analysis

Chapter 8 provided some insights into how to harness people's energy and gain their buy-in. That is one of the hardest things to do, particularly when faced with an organisational culture where people feel hard done by and don't really care about the higher level vision and goal. As I discussed in Chapters 2 and 3, the effect of silo working and tribalism on people's attitudes and willingness to change can be dire. Project managers often think they have gained the necessary agreement from local managers but then find the commitment and energy for change is not there on the part of the individual process users.

In Chapter 7 I hope I demonstrated the difficulty that an organisation would have achieving take-up and compliance to standardised processes if they lacked the capability maturity to manage these processes in a disciplined, consistent manner across the organisation. But some of the barriers to take-up and compliance seemed to come from the very nature of the change project itself. It is very rare, even in major transformation programmes, for the changes to affect everything people do in their jobs, across the whole organisation. We are usually dealing with just part of their workload – a piecemeal approach.

105

This is something I have not seen discussed in any change management books but which turns out to be a root cause of poor take-up and compliance. It stems from an inadequate focus at the discovery stage on making existing processes visible.

In most change projects, the first 'discovery' stage is to carry out an analysis of what is happening on the ground today and what needs to be improved. This will normally include an element of process mapping and workflow analysis. Quite often this is undertaken by external consultants and is quite superficial, perhaps involving selected managers, but perhaps not the staff who perform the tasks being changed. The project that then ensues focuses on introducing new systems and re-engineering the processes to gain the required improvement in efficiency and quality of performance, leaving anything that is outside the scope of the project more or less as it was.

Now if you examine any individual's job closely enough, particularly in a complex devolved service environment (and even more if the person doing the job has had time to mature and 'bed in' the processes), what often emerges is an organically grown, multi-layered mess. Each time new processes are introduced, the change project gets implemented and then staff are left to embed the changes into their routine. There is never time to go back and refine and retrain. So what happens? Everyone gets on and sorts out their own little ways of working, adding bits on as situations arise, accommodating change and responding to new demands: 'coping with the mess'.

Whenever a new requirement comes along, we seem to expect people to carry on coping with the mess, finding ways to fit the new processes in with those that have not been modified and modernised.

When I investigated this in one company, and asked some of the staff affected by the modernisation programmes what was actually

"We tried shoe-horning new systems into our old processes..."

"...it didn't work!"

happening as far as they saw it, I got two very strong messages back:

1. They are sick of having new processes foisted on them. As several people expressed it: "you can't just shoe-horn new processes on top of existing processes – it doesn't work". In fact it often created real problems – the new processes need to be brought in, people need training and time to learn and adapt, the new systems rarely work properly first time and never actually do everything they are supposed to do. So what happens? All the other stuff that wasn't included in the project gets delayed, people become overloaded and pressure mounts...

2. Years of piecemeal change had bred a new 'macho' culture into this workforce: people took pride in the fact that they are the only ones that can handle the 'mess'. Their managers don't know what is actually going on at the detailed level, a lot of what they do is not documented, but if they left "the place would collapse". This innate skill that people have to handle a complex set of untidy, flexible activities typically goes unrecognised, as a positive feature, by most process analysts. Their goal is, after all, to reduce this 'mess' to a clearly defined, well-planned smooth-running workflow.

So when consultants like me go into the analysis stage of a process change project, we often do not look in sufficient detail at the processes that are NOT being changed. We also under-estimate the level of this existing work, the amount of time and effort required to maintain it and the strange pride people take in being able to manage it, when planning the changes.

What happens is that, after going through a transformation experience once or twice, people's attitudes change. They begin to hide behind the need to keep the rest of the job going, reduce the priority given to making the required changes and find reasons why they can't comply fully. This 'it's my mess, leave it alone' attitude reinforces the barriers that are potentially there in any Structuralist culture and can prevent an organisation from moving up the organisational culture spiral.

What to do about it?

An effective solution is to carry out a more thorough and detailed initial analysis, fully involving the staff and to assign responsibility to someone to take all the existing processes that will not be directly affected and ask the three-part question:

- Do we need to carry on doing this?
- If so, does it have to be done by this team?
- If so, is there a more efficient way of doing it in the context of the other changes.

There is an extra cost involved in mapping processes at this detailed level (although with the use of rapid process mapping techniques and software tools, these costs can be kept to a minimum) but there are often real benefits in being able to apply LEAN[14] methods to the workflows and strip out unnecessary activity.

It is often the case that simplifying the way people work can bring real opportunities for releasing the resources needed to bring in the new processes. Analysis of an HR function in a government agency showed that many of their activities were being duplicated elsewhere in the organisation. Just acting on this released two people to work on the change initiative they were planning.

Another important reason for undertaking the analysis at this level of detail is that it can reveal some of the underlying causes of the inefficiency. Very often the reasons for doing things in a particular way have been lost in the mists of time. I have never seen this written up in any project management text-book, but a secret to tackling inefficiency is to look at the policies, not just at the processes.

If you dig deep enough, the root of an 'inefficient' process is usually a decision that was taken by someone, often no longer in the organisation, to deal with a situation or problem that may also no longer be current. When you look at the process itself, it is actually

---

[14] A method to eliminate duplication and waste in a workflow – comes from 'Lean manufacturing' techniques originated by Toyota in 1998 to get "the right things to the right place at the right time in the right quantity to achieve perfect work flow". It is now also widely applied in the service and IT sectors to any workflow improvement initative using these principles.

well-designed to achieve that policy efficiently and effectively – but the rationale for doing it may have disappeared or changed.

In some instances it is these out-of-date policies that govern expensive day-to-day processes and are costing the organisation in terms of inefficient use of resources, but nobody has had the data to challenge them. In one case I came across some pay and conditions contracts that were agreed long ago, probably for very good reasons – then. By assessing the cost of these against comparative pay and conditions in use elsewhere in the sector, I was able to quantify the cost of adhering to these policies. That was the ammunition needed to persuade the Finance Director to get them reviewed and changed.

So although there is an extra cost in carrying out detailed process mapping, it can deliver cost benefits in unexpected ways!

Note that I am not here advocating going on a cost-cutting mission. Setting out to cut costs as the main objective of a change project is usually counter-productive. It might work in the short term, but unless you have achieved a very good understanding of the processes and can identify in detail those that do not add any value, the consequences of cost-cutting can be unforeseen problems that will end up costing more. Experienced managers know that efficiency projects need to be, first and foremost, about improving the efficiency *and* the effectiveness of processes. The costs will come down when the processes are well-defined, well-managed and adopted by the people doing the work.

John O'Neil at AXA Ireland recognised this. His company did, in fact, streamline its processes – so much so that customers with a claim now have only two or three contacts with the insurance company after they have notified them, compared to the average of 18 in the 'bad old days'. But they did this through a programme of innovation, driven by the workforce and rewarded in the pay and bonus structure.

"It's not about setting out to cut costs..."

"When we changed how we worked, we needed fewer resources"

Gaining detailed process visibility brings another real benefit – understanding when work being carried out by staff or managers is not routine and therefore not as susceptible to process re-engineering.

The Capability Maturity Model works well for the routine, repeated processes seen in all organisations, such as financial transactions and regular information-gathering and reporting cycles.

It does not work so well for non-routine activity, such as ad hoc requests for information or the need to respond to new and fast-changing situations. But non-routine work can represent a significant proportion of the day-to-day activity in an organisation. And this type of work requires a different approach to recognise and respond to the requirement, undertake the task and produce the desired outcome.

The next chapter sets out a framework I have incorporated into the INPACT methodology that deals with non-routine work and the more complex processes involved. Applying a set of definitions to these aspects of an organisation's activity provides a route-map to the steps needed to include such work in change and efficiency improvement projects.

I have argued strongly for detailed mapping to make processes visible. I now want to return to the important role that process mapping and analysis plays in gaining people's ownership of change and ask the question: who should design the transformation?

The value of DIY process mapping

As a student of linguistics and child language learning, many years ago, I came across an intriguing fact: children do not learn language (or any other social behaviour) purely by imitation. They invent it for themselves, all over again, every time. Full of curiosity, they absorb what they hear and see around them and apply it to what they already know, until, by a process of differentiation and generalisation, they come up with approximately the same language (and social behaviour) as their parents and peer-group.

A further intriguing fact is that this need to develop our own version of the world around us is stronger than almost anything else in our human make-up – and it stays with us into adulthood.

As I became involved in process improvement and saw the problems that arose from superficial analysis, I also saw the opportunity to exploit some of this creative drive to gain the commitment and energy of the people who were going to use the new processes. Rather than developing and implementing the new processes in the traditional fashion (imposing them with the minimum of consultation) it is far more successful to work with the process users to carry out the analysis and to get *them* to evaluate the outputs of the process mapping exercise.

The creativity and innovation that this approach can unleash is significant and it allows you to establish clarity of purpose and direction in that part of the organisation that has to change the way they work. Even if you already know where you need to end up (e.g. a new system that has already been specified), by allowing the group to develop their own transition from the existing processes to the new ones – inventing their own route to the future – you will ensure that all the issues they know about at the detailed level are covered and that the new processes are 'fit for purpose'.

Another benefit: involving the operational team in mapping their own processes enables them to repeat their success in developing solutions in ongoing transformation programmes. This knowledge transfer is an important way to encourage innovation and continuous improvement.

Empowering local managers and staff to review, monitor and improve processes after the formal completion of the project can deliver significant ongoing benefits and embeds the culture change we need alongside the process improvements.

This approach not only delivers fully compliant processes, it shifts the culture up the spiral towards a more mature, empowered organisation, capable of managing change.

I came across an example of this in a recent project where a project management system was being upgraded so that managers could specify and monitor the tendering and contractual stages of their projects online. The primary purpose was to save administrative work for the procurement team and to give managers more responsibility for driving the process, but the organisation also recognised that the managers were already heavily overloaded, so it was essential that the design of the new system did not create even more work for them. To achieve this, the managers were consulted from the start of the development. But that was not sufficient to gain their support.

The new system needed to offer *them* real time savings as well.

A few months after the system came into operation, a review was carried out which sought managers' comments and suggestions. One of these focused not on the system but on the IT infrastructure on which it sat. It turned out that, with such a heavy workload, a lot of the managers were taking planning work home. However the project management system was not accessible via the internet, so they couldn't work on their project tenders and contracts. When the necessary IT links were put in place, take-up and usage of the system went up significantly. The planned savings were achieved, but more importantly, the managers felt in control of the way they were working and were happy to take more responsibility for driving the process.

I have focused a lot on the local operational people in an organisation. But many of the barriers to progress in an organisation come from middle and top management. Often the failure of a project can be traced back to the inability or unwillingness of senior management to lead and champion changes, or to police such changes when departments or specialist groups seek to opt out because 'we do things differently here'. The Organisational Culture model will enable you to judge whether this is a deep-seated organisational culture problem – in which case only personnel changes at the top will make a difference – or whether it might pay dividends to work to get stronger support from top management. Unless such weaknesses are addressed, any success will be temporary, as people will revert to old habits.

The same firm approach needs to be taken with external stakeholders (such as suppliers in an e-procurement project, or partners in a collaboration) to avoid an inter-dependency 'road-block'. That is more difficult, as you have even less control and influence over these stakeholders than over people in your own organisation. This is discussed again in the next chapter and in Chapter 17, 'Overcoming the Barriers to Success: the Action Plan'.

It is essential to put the effort in to identify and deal with these issues before embarking on the project, even if the methodology you plan to use to implement the project or programme does not make this preparation an overt activity. The best ones do, for example, Tabrizi's Rapid Transformation model has a Pretransformation phase. This is where the organisation recognises that it needs to change and takes the first steps to make it happen.[15]

So, the message in this chapter is that even when one is focused on process, it's the people that will bring about real improvement. Your approach must be geared to achieving culture change in the organisation as well as streamlining and modernising the way it works if you want high levels of take-up and compliance – an integrated approach.

So far in this book, I have dealt with process as if it was always routine and repeatable – which is the type of process that consultants love and the subject of most efficiency change projects.

But as I pointed out, not all processes are routine. In fact non-routine work can sometimes represent a significant proportion of the day-to-day activity in an organisation. The next chapter offers a framework that will enable you to include non-routine work in change projects.

---

[15] *Rapid Transformation: A 90-day Plan for Fast and Effective Change*, Harvard Business School Press, Behnam N. Tabrizi (November 2007)

10

Dealing with Complicated and Non-Routine Process

ORGANISATIONAL CAPABILITY

Culture → £ ← Process

THE PROJECT

Where the majority of an organisation's activities are routine, the performance of these processes can be assessed by looking at how well these processes are being managed and measured. Performance can be improved by applying conventional process re-engineering and LEAN principles to refine, streamline and automate these processes.

Of course, such process re-engineering must be coupled with sufficient attention to the organisational culture and the ownership of the changes involved, and to achieve good results one would need to understand and compensate for any immaturity of process management capability and lack of detailed process visibility. The standard INPACT approach.

But what if this approach doesn't work? What could be going on that would prevent such improvements?

One possible cause is the assumption that all the processes being addressed follow a routine pattern and are therefore susceptible to the change and improvement process described. This is almost certainly *not* the case. At least some of the work being undertaken will be more complicated than assumed and in extreme cases, the majority of the work may actually be **non-routine** – but that hasn't been recognised.

INPACT uses the Capability Maturity Model to assess an

organisation's process management capability in order to judge how well the organisation is likely to cope with process improvement and transformation. This approach works well for the routine, repeated processes seen in all organisations, such as financial transactions and regular information gathering and reporting cycles. It does not work so well for more complicated and non-routine activity, such as ad hoc requests for information or the need to respond to new and fast-changing situations. But complicated and non-routine work can represent a significant proportion of the day-to-day activity in an organisation.

Recognising this, I set out to find a model which would enable me to recognise when processes are complicated and non-routine, and to incorporate this into the INPACT methodology.

Non-routine work is driven by ad hoc and often fast-changing drivers – new customers, market downturns, press and public reaction to new products and services, new strategies and policy decisions, etc.

Just as the drivers of the processes are not the same all the time, so people's ways of coping with non-routine work will vary according to the circumstances. They develop non-standard processes and local work-arounds to meet the new requirements, often using the tacit expertise of the individuals involved to deal with the issue. Experts may be brought in to advise on the best approach – often from a manager's existing network of trusted associates and contacts. The CEO of a mining company that suffered from poor industrial relations found that when the union imposed a work-to-rule, it was "simply not possible to do business if everyone follows the rules" and he settled the dispute as quickly as he could.

If there are enough complicated and non-routine 'exceptions' in an organisation's activities, and if these and the value of the tacit knowledge and networks used to deal with them are overlooked or ignored in redesigning new systems, the process users will (rightly) dismiss the new systems as not fit for purpose and, as far as they are permitted to do so, carry on working the way they always have done. It's easier!

But incorporating the non-routine drivers and ways of dealing with them into improvement projects is a challenge beyond conventional process re-engineering and efficiency improvement methodologies. So a significant proportion of what gets done every day in an organisation remains in the 'too difficult' category for change and transformation projects to tackle.

How to overcome this shortcoming? First you need to be able to recognise non-routine activity and understand how it is being undertaken. The processes do not follow the logic of routine work:

Input (requirement) -> Process -> Output

The model I have adopted to describe and categorise the more complex processes involved in non-routine work is the Cynefin Framework.

The Cynefin Framework

Cynefin (pronounced kun-ev'in) is the name of a decision-making framework developed by David Snowden, Founder & Chief Scientific Officer of Cognitive Edge, and a knowledge management pioneer who has developed new methods and tools to assist organisations with truly complex problems and opportunities. (Cynefin is a Welsh word which, literally translated, means 'habitat' or 'place' but means far more – it also has a sense of one's multiple cultural, religious and geographic links to the past.)

The framework has five domains, characterised by the relationship between cause and effect. On the right are the two domains relating to routine or 'ordered' work: Simple and Complicated. On the left are the two domains relating to non-routine or 'un-ordered' work:

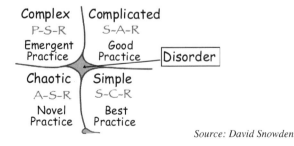

Source: David Snowden

Here's a summary of the domains and what they represent:

Routine (Ordered)

- **SIMPLE** (or Known) – the relationship between cause and effect is obvious. The approach is:

  Sense – Categorise – Respond

  So, when it is time to compile a monthly report, the manager goes to known sources of information, extracts the data, compiles the report and sends it to the known recipients. This type of routine activity represents much of the work carried out in organisations using repeatable processes and IT systems, so conventional management best practice, measurement and process improvement concepts apply.

- **COMPLICATED** (or Knowable) – the relationship between cause and effect requires investigation and analysis but the response can then be accommodated into a routine process. The approach is:

  Sense – Analyze – Respond

  COMPLICATED work has elements that are new each time, but within a defined knowledge and experiential domain, e.g. ad-hoc requests for information. Typically this will involve a level of added expertise to frame the response, so it is not possible to use a SIMPLE, standardised response process until that expertise has been consulted, but then it can be incorporated in the routine processes.

  The emphasis is, therefore, on 'who you know' with the knowledge to answer the question. If the organisation understands the nature of this activity and it is an important part of how it works, identifying and maintaining the body of expertise (inside or outside the organisation) will be part of its management good practice – and the consultation can be incorporated into routine process.

Non-Routine (Un-ordered)

- **COMPLEX** – the relationship between cause and effect can be identified in retrospect, but not in advance. An example would be where a trend or problem is manifesting itself but there is no clear reason. As the question cannot be articulated, there is no possibility of answering it by expert analysis or routine categorisation. The approach is:

  Probe – Sense – Respond

  This typically takes the form of putting a number of people or task forces to work on researching the trend or problem and coming up with hypotheses for the underlying cause/s, then experimenting until the hypothesis is found that seems to offer the best solution. David Snowden calls this *emergent* practice. In INPACT, this is embodied in the Systemist culture.

- **CHAOTIC** – there is no apparent relationship between cause and effect. This is where you suspect something might be going on but can't put your finger on it. The approach is:

  Act – Sense – Respond

  Intervention changes the underlying set of conditions and offers the opportunity to sense patterns – discovering the 'weak signals' in amongst the 'noise'. If these can be identified early enough, they can lead to what David Snowden calls *novel* practice. His pioneering work on developing and applying sense-making tools and techniques is aimed at addressing this Cynefin domain.

- **DISORDER** – the fifth domain, at the centre of the framework where the other four meet, is **DISORDER**. This is the state of not knowing what type of causality exists. Here, people will revert to their own comfort zone in making a decision.

In full use, the Cynefin framework also has sub-domains, and the boundary between SIMPLE and CHAOTIC is seen as a catastrophic one: complacency leads to failure. However, for the simple purpose of recognising the different types of activity and understanding the type of process being used to deal with these in an organisation, I have confined myself to the basic model – and principally to the first three categories: SIMPLE, COMPLICATED and COMPLEX.

INPACT and Cynefin

Applying the Cynefin Framework, you can now recognise that what I called 'routine' corresponds to the Cynefin model's SIMPLE and, with the additional 'Analyse' step, COMPLICATED categories.

If you think about your own organisation – and indeed your own role within the organisation – you will begin to see how little of your workload is truly SIMPLE. Apart from routine monthly performance and financial reporting cycles, very little is as simple as *Sense – Categorise – Respond*. But laid-down processes may not reflect this.

Having to consult an expert or bring in consultants before you can bring routine processes to bear on an issue or problem means you need to spend more time and cost to resolve it – more importantly it requires that you have identified the issue or problem as needing that expertise. An organisation whose senior people are fire-fighting rather than managing may be attempting to deal with COMPLICATED (*Sense – Analyze – Categorise – Respond*) and even COMPLEX (*Probe – Sense – Respond*) situations and trying to fit them into SIMPLE processes.

The result is that the unrecognised non-standard cases escalate into crises, which take up even more time to resolve, perpetuating the fire-fighting cycle. If scrutiny, time and resources are not applied to understanding the underlying causes, such situations remain unresolved and eventually may cause significant damage to the organisation.

You will recall from Chapter 7 that it is very easy to underestimate the complexity of a change project. One of the insights I got from learning about Cynefin was the realisation that change

119

moves even SIMPLE processes into the COMPLEX domain, because we are projecting them into the unpredictable future – adding a new dimension. Much of the work of the change consultant therefore comprises using the COMPLEX approach: *Probe – Sense – Respond*: probe to identify patterns that one can make sense of, then develop strategies to deal with them and propose appropriate solutions. Interestingly, these can often be surprisingly simple (if I have done my work right!)

Route-map to integrate non-routine processes into change projects

Applying Cynefin principles to the organisation's activities can provide a useful route-map to bringing complicated and non-routine work successfully into change and efficiency improvement projects.

Where an apparently SIMPLE repeatable process actually has to handle COMPLICATED or COMPLEX exceptions, designing a system to manage these may be possible, but only if you recognise them and are able to successfully exploit the tacit knowledge and expertise needed to provide the correct response.

An essential first step to understanding the mix of work types is to carry out a knowledge management audit, with the specific remit to uncover the extent to which the work being undertaken by management and staff is being processed using SIMPLE, COMPLICATED or COMPLEX responses.

The table overleaf briefly describes the three types of work as an aid to recognising them in a knowledge audit.

Look for the response types in the analysis:

SIMPLE: **Sense –** **Categorise –** **Respond**	The process will be overt and repeated. In an organisation where business process capability is at Level 1 or above, the process will have a name and basic management controls will be in place. In more mature organisations, you should find process maps, management of compliance and efficiency measures. The trick is to identify what is NOT actually SIMPLE – which requires detailed visibility of the processes.
COMPLICATED: **Sense – Analyze** **– Categorise –** **Respond**	Where business process capability is at Level 2 or below, it is unlikely that the process will be recognised and managed particularly well. Staff will be doing this work outside of, and in addition to, the 'mainstream' processes; managers will probably be spending much of their time on this type of work, but it won't be managed or measured. Even if a knowledge management audit has been carried out and a knowledge management strategy put in place, it is unlikely that the use of tacit knowledge and networks will have been included.
COMPLEX: **Probe – Sense –** **Categorise –** **Respond**	This activity is often undertaken as senior management-sponsored task force projects and enquiries. Organisations with business process capability at Level 3 and below that make use of these approaches tend to regard them as additional to the 'day job'. They form no part of the processes when change and improvement initiatives are undertaken. Indeed, the change and improvement initiatives themselves are often carried out in this way – completely outside and in parallel to the conventional definition of 'what we do'.

The level of COMPLICATED work is often associated with the nature of the organisation – a civil service organisation will typically be responding to government policy changes, public enquiries and outcomes of research; a retail organisation will be responding to market take-up, competitive pressures, changes in the regulatory environment etc.

I have left aside the CHAOTIC category, as it is unlikely that you will encounter activity of this type in assessing and managing organisational change and efficiency projects. A CHAOTIC situation requires immediate and decisive action – there's no time to consult and no point in analysing. This is the domain where charismatic and strong leadership works best. (But beware – this crisis management style is addictive and can become a dominant style for the organisation – a recipe for disaster!)

There may be an underlying sense among senior managers that 'we don't know what we don't know', in which case I would refer you to Cognitive Edge's powerful work on how to make sense of unstructured data – but that lies far beyond the scope of this book.

Strategies for dealing with COMPLICATED and COMPLEX processes

1. Separation and reorganisation

It may be that the mix is such that the system cannot sensibly accommodate it – the instances of COMPLICATED work are too high or the variety is too great. In these circumstances, systems would need to be unreasonably complex and expensive to cope. It is more practical to **separate** SIMPLE and COMPLICATED workflows – a valuable first stage in redesigning the processes.

Look for sets of repeated triggers of COMPLICATED work. There may be a regular stream of ad hoc requirements or enquiries, all slightly different but which, when aggregated, form a definable workload for specific people. For example, requests for information coming from different sources and through a number of channels but which all require fairly urgent attention.

It is likely that the way this activity is handled is different in each case and no attempt has been made to understand the patterns of work or manage the outputs so that the knowledge gained is available after the event.

If this is so, it would be ideal if you could reorganise roles and responsibilities to segregate the COMPLICATED work. That might not be possible in practice – in most organisations, everyone has at least a small element of COMPLICATED work. However, if at least some of this workload could be managed in a more efficient way, you will see benefits in time and scarce resources saved.

2. Standardisation

Although each occurrence of COMPLICATED work may require a unique *Sense – Analyze – Respond* approach, the process of **identifying and involving the expert** may be capable of being standardised and made a SIMPLE process. A good knowledge management strategy will include mapping the tacit knowledge and networks of associates and valued contacts for each key member of the team. In more mature organisations (Level 3 Organisational Culture and above) this knowledge will be seen as a vital asset and made overt and more widely accessible.

Similarly, **recording the outcome** of a COMPLICATED activity can be done using a standard format and following a standard process, so that the knowledge can be captured, categorised, stored and made available for possible re-use in similar situations by other members of the organisation. In my civil service example, all Ministers' questions should be logged, a standard process used for consulting the experts, all responses then brought back into a standard and SIMPLE process for distributing the information, categorising and storing it in an accessible format. Another, similar process should be implemented for all Press enquiries etc.

Don't forget, COMPLICATED processes are still within the Routine or 'Ordered' domains – they are just harder to deal with because they demand specific and varied consultation action at the front end of the process.

Standardising the way you handle these – finding patterns you can repeat – increases the overall value of the knowledge held in the organisation and potentially reduces the level of expensive COMPLICATED work, increasing cost-efficiency.

3. A Systems approach

Another strategy is taken by followers of the systems approach to performance improvement, as espoused by John Seddon, the originator of 'systems thinking' in service industries. He and his fellow systems engineering disciples claim that efficiency comes from designing systems around "economies of flow" rather than economies of scale. So an organisation's systems and processes need to be designed from the outside in – i.e. customer-centric – rather than based on efficiency, as measured by conventional performance targets.

These systems put more emphasis on up-skilling and empowering front-line staff to deal with COMPLICATED as well as SIMPLE customer 'traffic' (enquiries, sales orders, complaints, requests for information etc). While this increases the costs of customer handling, the claim is that it is less than the true cost of dealing with the repeat traffic caused by a failure to deal with the customer to their satisfaction, first time around.

The Systems community argues that people's behaviour is a product of the system you put them in, which seems perfectly reasonable to me. People are not naturally idle and devious, it's the command-and-control approach to management that assumes they are – and so they become so. They don't stop caring about the customers' needs, it's the performance targets they work to, that will create that culture.

Think back to the Systemist culture in our model and the recognition in that culture of the complex, multi-faceted needs and attitudes of each individual – employee, team member, caring about the customer, part of a community.

Recognising these multiple aspects and honouring them can be the key to unlocking their motivation and creativity. Forcing them into a target-driven regime is definitely *not* the way to achieve their best performance.

The example given in Chapter 5 illustrates and validates John Seddon's approach: the service organisation that was using CRM without the right balance between process and cultural capability was generating more work, as customers were repeatedly ringing to chase for an answer. The cost of resourcing this additional workload was actually higher than giving frontline staff the time and the skills to deal with the requests and complaints when they first came in. John Seddon's approach would be to design the system from the outside in – customer focused – and set customer satisfaction targets, rather than time-to-answer performance targets.

This example illustrates the importance of getting the balance right between process and people. Empowering people to use clever technology is the key to successful management of any SIMPLE process and, it seems, to handling COMPLICATED workflows.

Brendon Riley, Chief Executive of IBM UK[16], said: "We can make smarter decisions now. It is possible to infuse intelligence into the systems and processes by which we work. It is about empowering decision-making with the right information at the right time in areas where human judgement is critical".

That ties in well with the INPACT philosophy. An organisation which has an aligned and empowered workforce is likely also to be able to manage standardised and efficient processes, which are being used consistently by everyone to achieve high levels of customer satisfaction – i.e. effectively.

By contrast, if the organisation is inward-looking and bureaucratic, as is typical of a Structuralist culture, its people will be focused on meeting imposed, departmental performance targets, rather than working together to meet the needs of their customers.

You only have to compare organisations which have empowered their people with those that measure and control every aspect of the workflow to notice the fundamental difference in pace, enthusiasm and sense of shared purpose that comes across from the moment you walk into their offices.

Unsurprisingly, INPACT embodies the Systems approach in the

---

[16] *The Times*, 17th March 2009

Systemist culture which recognises that to change people's behaviour, one must work on changing both how the organisation manages its people *and* its systems and processes. As I outlined in Chapter 3, a Systemist manager doesn't try to impose order in what is, in effect a COMPLEX context. He or she sets the direction and looks to the team to work out what to do to get there, often encouraging several parallel approaches to find out the one that works best.

Applying the Cynefin Framework allows us to recognise the nature of the activity in an organisation and provides a useful understanding of the different processes used to deal with COMPLICATED and COMPLEX work, alongside the SIMPLE work that is the stuff of conventional process mapping and redesign.

From this more sophisticated analysis, one can develop a route-map for including such non-routine work into change and efficiency improvement projects. Whether you extend this to the relatively radical systems approach advocated by John Seddon, reorganise to manage the COMPLICATED work in a more efficient way or simply recognise the COMPLEX nature of the problem and allow enough time and consultation to achieve results, the insights provided by Cynefin will help to drive the change and improvement process.

The next chapter looks at trust – an essential ingredient if you want people to travel with you on the transformation journey – and how to measure it.

11

Measuring Trust & the Trust/Cost Relationship

Trust is the 'oil' that helps people to accept change in an organisation. It empowers them to remove the barriers that block change, with a minimum of friction. (That's why having a highly visible senior manager at change project meetings is so important – they don't even have to say anything!)

An absence of trust between managers and staff and between parts of an organisation will slow down and even stop a project. The higher the levels of distrust, the more time and effort the project will require and the higher the cost. So if you could measure trust in the group that is to be affected by a change project, you could develop a useful predictor of the additional time and cost involved in implementing that change project.

I looked in vain for an approach that would allow me to measure trust. Stephen Covey Jr wrote a useful book about "The Speed of Trust – The One Thing that Changes Everything"[17] but one thing he failed to do in that book was to suggest ways to measure trust – and other authorities on the subject shed no more light.

---

[17] *The Speed of Trust – The One Thing that Changes Everything*, Stephen M.R. Covey (2006)

So I dreamt up my own approach. How does one measure trust? By asking a few key questions...

There are essentially three key relationships anyone has in an organisation:

1. Relationship with my manager
2. Relationship with my staff
3. Relationship with my peers

That gives a three-dimensional model:

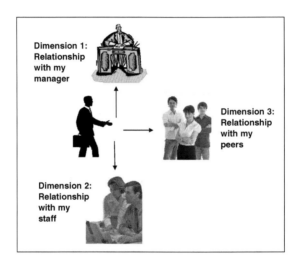

For each dimension, I will use a four-point scale to score the relationship:

3 = excellent relationship – high levels of trust and respect
2 = quite good relationship, reasonable levels of trust and respect
1 = poor relationship, low levels of trust and respect
0 = non-existent relationship, no trust or respect.

Now using a simple questionnaire – see overleaf – I elicit the responses from a sample of the people involved in the change project. Adding up the scores for the three questions gives a maximum score of 9.

Measuring Distrust Questionnaire

Q1. My team works:	[Scoring]
Totally without my intervention – they will come to me if they need me	3
Without my intervention under normal circumstances, for routine work	2
I need to keep my eye on them	1
Unless I am on them constantly, nothing gets done	0
Q2. My manager represents my interests well, consults me when necessary and keeps me fully informed about any changes that might affect me, my job or my area of responsibility	
Totally	3
Mostly	2
Not too confident about this	1
Not at all – I have to find stuff out through the grapevine	0
Q3. I have a good relationship with my peer group – other managers at my level in the organisation. We share information and ideas and they keep me informed about any changes that might affect me, my job or my area of responsibility	
Totally	3
Mostly	2
Not too confident about this	1
Not at all – I have to find this out through the grapevine	0

Turn this into a percentage (so 9 = 100%). That gives a measure of the level of trust. Now deduct that from 100 to obtain the % of distrust – because it is the *shortfall* in trust that I need to apply as an incremental factor to the time and cost of implementation in the project's business plan.

So, if the score is 3, that gives me a trust % of 33%. Deducting that from 100 gives a measure of distrust of 67%. Applying this measure to a project with a planned roll-out of 1 year and an implementation cost of £40,000 would add 8 months and around £27,000 to the cost, significantly affecting the projected ROI (return on investment).

In my experience, this seems to correlate well with what happens in practice – the lower the level of trust, the longer it takes to implement the projects and gain the benefits, as illustrated:

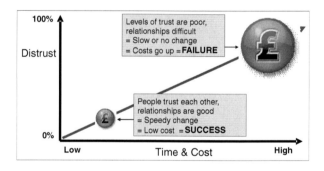

Why is there such a strong relationship between trust and implementation time/cost? If you think about the implementation process, it's obvious:

- If I trust and respect you and you ask me to do something, I am likely to do it if I can. Under these circumstances, the 'transaction cost' of the request is **1** and the result is **1** – i.e. it's done, quickly and at little cost.

- If our relationship is not as good and I ignore your request, the 'transaction cost' is **1** but you have a result of **0**.

130

- So you repeat the request and I still don't give it any priority. Which means the 'transaction cost' goes up to **2**, but you still have a result of **0**.

- Finally, you escalate the request. Having failed to get anywhere by asking me, you get your boss involved. He/she passes it to my boss, who orders me to comply, a 'transaction cost' of **3** – so now the cumulative transaction cost is **6**, before you get your result of **1**.

Every additional communication transaction means time and effort has to be expended, which costs money (and more as it escalates up the management tree), but an even greater cost will be the delay to the completion of the project and the inability to gain the planned benefits within the planned timescale.

There will always be an element of distrust in relationships, but the more mature the organisation's culture, the more networking and sharing that goes on between people, the less of a barrier this becomes. And it can be critical to the success of a change project to build up this trust between key stakeholders.

When you have collected the data, look for patterns in the responses, as this will often provide clues to 'fault-lines' that bear further investigation. In earlier chapters I quoted the situation in an NHS hospital trust, where even though there was general agreement that something had to be done to reduce costs, the INPACT assessment confirmed such a degree of distrust and lack of respect that an initiative to standardise medical purchasing was completely stalled. When I looked at the pattern of response, the major 'fault-line' was between the clinical and non-clinical managers.

If you see that distrust has the potential to jeopardise your project, it is important to deal with it, for instance by bringing together process users and stakeholders from across the organisation into a Change Team. Make sure you cover all three dimensions of the relationships between the people involved in the change.

Facilitate dialogue and co-operation to enable individuals to feel they are contributing to the change process. This should encourage the development of trust.

If the levels of trust and respect in the organisation (or that part being affected by the change project) are really poor or non-existent, you may have to gain senior management awareness of the problem and initiate a programme to build better relationships across the stakeholder groups, before you embark on the change project itself. In extreme cases, clever psychology and subterfuge may be the only way forward!

The solution in the NHS case was to exploit the national drive to improve patient safety, rather than focusing on cost-saving, thus bypassing the area of conflict. It was recommended that a standardisation panel should be set up, championed by the CEO and sponsored by the Finance Director, but led by the Safety Improvement Manager and populated entirely by Clinical Managers and Consultants, with the procurement group only providing a secretariat function, working in the background to identify best value products for trial and putting contracts in place. Although the recommendation was accepted, such is the pace of change in that organisation that I am still waiting to see it happen…

External Stakeholders

External stakeholders are those people or organisations over whom you have no authority, only (hopefully) some influence. Typically these will include: customers, suppliers, project partners and other organisations working contractually or collaboratively with you. In large corporate groups or multi-divisional or departmental organisations, external stakeholders may be companies, divisions or departments sitting within your organisation, but outside your senior manager's direct control.

The impact of external stakeholder non-cooperation on project timescales can be significant. They can hold up projects and even stop them altogether. You have no power over their actions, so can do little more than try to influence them. If their priorities are different from yours, there may be little you can do about it. Conversely, there may be occasions when the external stakeholder can be a project manager's greatest ally, reinforcing the case for adequate resources or adding weight to arguments for mandating changes.

If the relationship with external stakeholders is critical to the success of the project, a good level of trust needs to be established ahead of the project being planned. If this foundation of trust is not there, it will be difficult – perhaps impossible – to engage them and get their co-operation to make the necessary changes when the project is being implemented.

A well-planned and executed consultation and communication programme, carried out in the initial project planning stage will help to build this trust and ensure that they are ready and willing to accept the changes when the project is implemented. Communication with external stakeholders needs to emphasise the benefits – the 'what's in it for me?' factor – wherever possible. This communication needs to continue throughout the project, ramping up as the system is rolled out, to encourage take-up and compliance.

If you are doubtful about your ability to secure a trust relationship with key external stakeholders, reconsider the project's scope and ambitions, assess the potential risk on timescales and take-up and modify the implementation plan accordingly.

Collaborative projects are prime examples where dealing well with these considerations is of critical importance – and the trend is towards more collaboration and therefore more of our working relationships spanning the traditional boundaries. Even suppliers are now increasingly becoming integrated into the fabric of organisations in a bid to speed up and improve the quality of product and service delivery.

With the pace of change getting ever faster, organisations have to respond in days, not months, to new situations. So they need to be able to call upon their partners, collaborators and suppliers as well as their own people to make sure they deliver what the customer needs – and this applies to public sector 'customers' as much as it does in the competitive business context.

Poor relationships will hinder this – and may even stop it happening at all.

David Noble, CEO of CIPS (Chartered Institute of Purchase & Supply) said it well: "Relationships will become core as internal hierarchy gives way to a network of skills and the external market [gives way] to a network of partnerships"[18]

Carrying out an INPACT assessment of culture and business process capability on key partners, collaborators and suppliers will give a very good indication of where the barriers to trust and good relationships lie and what needs to be done to overcome them.

Take the housing association I mentioned in Chapter 3, whose CEO was concerned that the other organisations had different styles of management and might have lower levels of capability. Trust in his association was high and people communicated well across the organisation. Everyone had direct access to the CEO if there was something they wanted to discuss or alert him to. This contrasted with the silo culture in the other organisations which meant that groups tended to keep information to themselves and only communicated upwards by means of formal reports. The CEOs were visible to some extent in all of the companies but none operated a similar open-door policy.

Poor levels of trust and lack of respect, between management and staff, between colleagues and between external stakeholders, breeds inertia, which is an big component of the Cost of Change, on the right hand side of the change equation in Chapter 8 – one of the 'boulders we have to push up the hill' to achieve movement and change in organisations.

The next chapter looks at another area of distrust and resistance and another component of this Cost of Change. It is our relationship with technology.

---

[18] David Noble, CEO, CIPS at a CIPS London Branch meeting, June 2009

12

Why We Resist Technology and What to Do About It

Resistance to change is endemic – it is the way we are made. Change represents risk and we are risk-averse. Resistance to change when it is related to the use of modern technology is even greater. By technology I mean anything that uses the power of computing: equipment in the home, on the road and in the office, automated business processes, communications systems etc.

So this resistance can include a manager's disinclination to taking up the newly-introduced project management software, the time it has taken for organisations to accept chip-and-pin banking, or my inability to correctly programme the DVD recorder (thank goodness for the Sky box!)

All of these have one thing in common, they require that you adapt to a new and unfamiliar way of doing things, governed by an apparently alien and frightening technology. It is this last bit – 'alien and frightening technology' – that is the root of the real opposition to technology-based change.

But we all use technology, all the time. We are surrounded by it. I am sitting in a centrally heated house at a comfortable temperature, thanks to a thermostat and time-switch, sitting on an ergonomically-designed chair (or so the designers would have me believe!) using a computer to write this book. Even the clothes I am wearing owe their fibre composition and cut to technology.

At the office, we use computer systems, email and voice communications technology without pausing each time to think: "I am using technology". The resistance that you might have once had to using a new system or changing over to using emails instead of fax and telephone has long since dissipated.

The point is that once you are familiar with the technology, you take it for granted. This has its positive side: you don't think twice about driving your car, even though it is probably the most sophisticated piece of equipment you have. But it also has its negative side: when your car goes wrong and you have to pay for a garage to link it up to a diagnostic computer and charge you the earth for putting it right, *that's* when you notice how sophisticated its technology is!

In other words, well-designed technology, when it works, becomes invisible. When it doesn't, it becomes an expensive and time-wasting pain in the neck!

Our relationship with technology is complex. Ask someone about it and they will position themselves somewhere along a spectrum: at one end are a small group which I will label "Love new technology". This group is, apparently, predominantly male and under 30, although I am sure that women and the older generations of technophiles are represented too! These are the gadget-lovers, the early adopters of anything new and shiny that beeps at you, the people who spend hours at work finding ways to improve (or crash) new equipment and programmes.

I call these people the 'super-users'. At home, it's usually the kids who can show you how to programme the new TV. At work it's important to know who to ask when you have to create a new financial report for the first time or need to remember how to set up a spreadsheet pivot table. Ideally, this 'expert' will be a business person who is skilled in using the technology, not a 'techie' who is uninterested in solving real business problems.

At the other extreme are the "Hate new technology" group, predominantly female, I'm reliably informed, but with a good number of men over 40, for whom the new technology has become baffling and 'unnecessary' (to quote one member of this group!).

Members of the 'Hate new technology' group wish everything could be simpler. They resent the time and effort it takes to learn new tricks, to change habits and adapt perfectly good ways of doing things to accommodate the dictates of a new piece of equipment or software application. They usually have a good horror story of an encounter with new technology to justify their antipathy.

But go back and look at this group once the new technology has been absorbed into the daily routine. Ask my elderly mum, 3 weeks after I had to almost physically force her to use her new microwave; ask the hospital nurse who spent months refusing to learn how to use the computer to save her writing down every bandage and suture pack she used. Ask them then – and they will look at you as if you are mad. "What technology?" they will reply.

Well-designed and reliable technology, once adopted, very quickly becomes familiar enough to become invisible. The new CRM (customer response management) system, installed recently in the offices of the online plumber's merchant I use, took ages to install and bring up to the required call handling capacity and created a great deal of griping and grumbling in the ranks of the customer services staff I had the need to speak to. But 3 months later, the calls were answered faster, a cheerful voice at the other end of the phone suggested that everyone had settled into the new system – and my enquiry about the new system was met with a puzzled pause – why did I want to talk about that?

(By the way, we should feel a little bit sorry for the IT industry – they get blamed for the computer crashes and system failures but they never get praised when the technology does work!)

So how do you get people past the resistance to this point of familiarity? There are no short cuts. Familiarity only comes with a (sometimes considerable) personal investment of time and effort. It requires sufficient exposure to the technology that the benefit, not the operation of the new technology, becomes uppermost in the mind. But you can help it along the way. In a recent example, the Estates manager in an organisation was considering acquiring a new Asset

Management system. I gave him the following advice:

1. Firstly, selecting the right technology is critical to the success of any IT-related change project. This means: being good at saying what you want, being good at buying it right and ensuring that you get what you needed. That's a subject that could take up a whole other book, but have a look at Chapter 13 for some key questions to ask. In this example, I helped them articulate what they needed, which was a bit different from what the Estates manager was being 'sold' by enthusiastic suppliers.

2. Make sure as far as possible that the equipment or software application is intuitive and easy to use. If necessary, hide it – designers have long understood that a simple black box is less scary than a complicated looking device with wires coming out of it! In my example, one proposed system was so difficult to use that staff joked they needed a pilot's licence! Don't emphasise the technology, emphasise the benefits. If you are introducing a system to automate a process so that people have less work to do, that's what you first talk to them about – their reduced workload. Don't show them screen shots or try to explain the technology. That comes later. And please don't do what the Estates manager did – he sent out the supplier's enthusiastic salesman to demonstrate all the features of the technology to his staff. He nearly lost the project there and then!

3. Wherever possible involve the end-user in the decision-making. In Chapter 9 I showed how important it is to have people mapping the new processes and inventing their own route to the future. I suggested this for the Asset Management system, which was going to fundamentally change a number of people's roles in that property department. Doing this gave them access to the technology in a 'safe' environment, generated some degree of ownership of the changes they had to make and helped to ensure subsequent take-up of the new processes and systems.

4. Introduce the change with a well-planned communications and

training programme. Remember, familiarity comes with time and exposure to the technology. The Estates manager identified two 'early adopters', younger members of the group who were quite keen on the new system. They showed by example that it was not so hard to learn the new tricks and gain the benefits. I suggested that the training provided by the supplier had to be appropriately tailored to the target audience, not 'out of a box' and that worked well.

5. Don't just rely on the Help function, even if it does have an online self-teach tutorial. Timing is everything – arrange the training so that the learning can be applied immediately. It's no good training people two months before the technology is introduced – it will all be forgotten. If implementation gets delayed and that does happen, put on a short refresher programme.

6. Provide ongoing support as the technology is absorbed. This is usually ignored, as it introduces extra cost and the experts are usually needed elsewhere, but most of the real benefits in my example came when people had got used to the technology and started to be creative: "Can it do this?" It's worth having an expert around to coach and encourage this process. We ensured that the supplier provided a support person who came in every few months – and one of the team soon become 'Mr Super-user', making small adjustments to how they used the system that actually generated significant savings over the following months.

Overcoming people's natural resistance to adopting new technology is at the heart of achieving organisational transformation and the effort needed to keep pushing the boulder up the hill can be overwhelming. It's no surprise that maintaining the momentum – this 'push' dynamic – of some change projects has proved too hard for low capability organisations.

So is there a better way?

Perhaps...

13

How Robust Is Your IT Plan? Five Key Questions to Ask

Selecting the right information and communications technology[19] is not like buying anything else. It seems to affect everyone but be understood by no-one. It costs more than you thought it would, takes longer to make it work then you expected and does less than you wanted. But still everyone tells you – you must have the latest computers, software and communications systems if you want to keep up with your competition.

IT enables change and most change projects have an IT component. Automation of key processes can bring significant benefits: scalability, speed, increased accuracy, improved efficiency, better management information etc. But it can also bring disaster. I have already identified one risk – dependency on the new technology to achieve the benefits, rather than recognising that it's the USE of the technology by staff and managers to 'change the way we work'. Technology-led projects are still common, despite everything that has been written and said about the subject.

Here are some key questions that every organisation should

---

[19] Strictly this should be abbreviated to ICT, but on this occasion I will follow the herd and shorten it to IT.

answer before investing in IT. This was originally written mainly for smaller organisations which do not have the skills and experience to plan, implement and exploit IT for competitive advantage. However, over the years, it has been my experience that even the larger organisations need to go back to basics once in a while to ask themselves these questions.

As you work through the questions, score the responses in a simple High = 3 / Medium = 2 / Low = 1 framework.

1. Are you focusing on the business benefits?

Introducing IT into your mainstream activities? Or making significant changes to the systems you are using? Have you thought about your own business, how it operates and what makes it successful, before you start? The cupboards are littered with solutions that have never been used or fallen into disuse because people jumped too quickly to focus on the technology. It's easy to do. And a failure to focus on your competitive strengths when you introduce IT could mean you risk damaging your business.

2. Do you understand the technology?

You also need the skills in-house to understand the IT available, how to exploit it for business benefit and what it will *not* do. Then you need to have the capability to put this information to good use.

How does your organisation score on this?

3. Are you good at saying what you want?

Once you are sure that you have focused on the business objectives, not the technology, in your plans, you still have the big hurdle of specifying your requirements.

If you are lucky, you will have someone in the company who has the experience and understanding of IT to help you carry out this analysis, but it's usually down to local managers in the end to understand and specify exactly what it is they want the new system to do – in terms of your business, not the technology, and focusing on 'must-haves', not 'would-likes'.

4. Do you trust your people to innovate?

Implementing a new system is a learning experience, for you and for anyone in your company who uses the system. Remember, the initial reasons for starting down this path may not be the ones that give you the real benefits in the end. So trust your people to experiment – they will find innovative ways of using the new facilities which you never expected (especially if they are under 25!). But do develop a properly managed way of introducing these ongoing changes into your business – if you don't, chaos will reign.

5. Do you trust your suppliers to deliver?

Satisfy yourself that the suppliers you have chosen can deliver solutions that work. Never believe a promise – always ask for a demonstration that simulates as nearly as possible the conditions in your business.

It is key to success to develop a good relationship with the suppliers who sold you the components of your new system. With any luck you will need to upgrade and expand the system to meet the new demands as your business grows and you will need their help to exploit the opportunities you have created.

Put your scores into a table and see what it suggests about how well you are managing this important part of the project.

Remember, High = 3, Medium = 2 and Low = 1.

Add up the scores. The maximum is 15 and anything above 12 can be regarded as 'High' as an overall score. If you have scored 'High', overall, you can probably have some confidence that the IT will go in okay and will do what it is supposed to do.

If you scored 8-12 (Medium overall) that suggests that it would be worth paying more attention to those areas that let your score down.

Anything less than 8 (Low overall) and you should really review whether the project should go ahead.

Here's an example of a construction plant hire company that was implementing a new planning system that affected their core business activity – it was critical to improving their ability to get the right plant to the customer's site on time.

Question	
1. Focus on business benefits	2
2. Understand the technology	1
3. Good at saying what you want	2
4. Trust people to innovate	1
5. Can you trust supplier	3
Overall	9

The company's specification showed that they had understood the need to focus on business benefits but this was not confirmed when talking to the IT manager whose responsibility it was to bring in the new system. It also became clear in that discussion that the system they had chosen was the Managing Director's preference, not the IT manager's. They had consulted their staff and shown them what the new system would do – and some of the specific requirements in the specification came from that discussion – but there was no sense that the staff would have the time or opportunity to explore the capabilities of the new software – the roll-out plan was very tight and the MD expected everyone to be using it instead of the current manual processes with a week of installation. This was mitigated by the positive response from the solution supplier, who was clearly very experienced in working in this sector and confident that they could support a rapid switch-over.

With a score of 9, just above the Low threshold, this project was risky.

In the event, the IT manager took the initiative to spend a day with the supplier learning about the system, so that he could train the staff himself. He also ensured that the plant inventory and job data files were up-to-date and ready to be loaded into the planning system. Finally, during the initial period while the supplier was still involved, he initiated a number of changes which increased the usability of the system and gave the staff access to features they hadn't realised were available but which reduced their workload.

Selection of the right technology, appointment of capable and reliable suppliers and sound management of the planning and implementation can be the key to a successful project. However I repeat: the IT solution is only the tool – it is not, in itself, the solution to the problem that is driving the need for change. A recent critical report by the Joseph Rowntree Reform Trust on the state of the government's 46 databases expressed this brilliantly:

> *"If you think IT is the solution to your problem, then you don't understand IT and you don't understand your problem either."*[20]

I couldn't have said it better myself.

---

[20] 'Database State', Joseph Rowntree Reform Trust report, March 2009

14

The Pull Dynamic of a Benefits Realisation Plan

Ask project managers what the most difficult and time-consuming part of their job is and they will tell you – getting people to make the changes that are needed to achieve the outcomes of the project. This is often expressed as: "communicate, communicate, communicate".

The problem lies in the assumption that change is something that is 'done to you' – the 'push' dynamic that operates in almost all the projects I have seen, or been part of, over the years. This chapter proposes an alternative approach.

One of the common features of an IT-based change project is the difficulty in identifying, quantifying and demonstrating the benefits, particularly where these are indirect. An example is the 15 minutes per day that can be saved by automating a process that affects 200 people in an organisation. This theoretically releases over 16 man-hours of resources a day – equivalent to about two people who could be redeployed to improve productivity, but because this 'saving' is distributed across a lot of people, it disappears into a black hole.

I have seen many business cases for such projects which claim these time savings as cashable benefits. In most cases they are there to boost the return on investment figures, which for infrastructure projects, tend to look pretty weak. The reality is that most

145

organisations do not have the time or discipline to follow up and check whether the benefits have been realised. So the only way to ensure the benefits are actually achieved is to cut department budgets to reflect the theoretical improvement and leave it to the local staff and managers to cope. Over time, this simply puts managers under so much pressure that they cut corners and the quality of performance goes down.

I was having a discussion with a project manager who was moaning about this – he asked: "Isn't there a better way of doing this?" You probably will have realised by now that asking me a question like that is like showing a red rag to a bull!

I thought back to a project I had heard about when I was running a 'best practice' group. This was a major telephone network company who had created a sophisticated Benefits Realisation process, whereby local managers were held accountable for the changes in their part of the organisation. In that project, the focus was not on the indirect 'savings' but on core performance improvement, enabled by the new system they were implementing. The process was far too ambitious and complicated to introduce into most projects, but it made me think that a similar approach suitably simplified might work.

It did. Indirect 'savings', already discredited by many project managers, were no longer the focus, management of performance improvement was. And then I found that this approach had an unexpectedly positive effect. It changed the dynamics of a project from 'push' to 'pull'. Let me explain.

You will recall the question: 'Who is responsible for realising the benefits from your change project?' And the answer: *'The operational managers and staff who will be using the new system/process.'*

So why is that the change always seems to be being PUSHED on these managers and staff by the Project Manager? Wouldn't it be better if the changes were being PULLED by the operational managers and staff?

That's what the Dynamic Benefits Realisation model helps us to do.

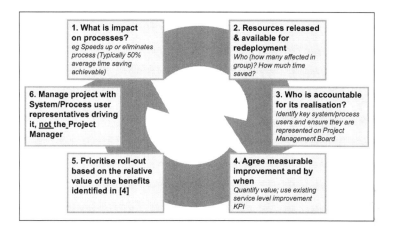

The model has 6 steps:

1.   **Open a dialogue** with the managers of teams that are expected to be affected by the change project. Agree with these managers what the impact of the proposed change is likely to be on their team. For example, the new system might speed up or even eliminate a process. (As a benchmark, on average the automation of a manual process achieves roughly 50% efficiency improvement, i.e. it releases this time for use on other work.)

2.   **Quantify** the level of resources that would be released and available for redeployment in each manager's team. Who are they, how many are affected, how much time would be saved?

3.   **Explore** with the managers what this released resource could be used for. What Key Performance Indicator (KPI) targets are they already being measured against where they are under pressure to improve performance? Discuss the likely timescales for achieving these improvements, based on when the new system/process is planned to be available.

NB use an *existing* service level improvement performance indicator wherever possible.

4. **Establish accountability** – ensure that the managers are included as User Representatives on the Project Management Board (a good PRINCE2 principle, for those who use that methodology!). Ensure that they are accountable to the management board for the performance improvement targets you have negotiated.

5. **Prioritise** the roll-out of your project based on the relative value of the benefits identified in [4].

6. **Implement** the project, ensuring that the User Representatives play an active role in driving it forward to enable them to meet their commitments to the board.

Using this approach, you change the dynamics of the project. Provided the organisation has a reasonably mature business process capability (i.e. regular performance management reporting), the User Representative managers will be held accountable for the improvements they have agreed to, and should be banging on *your* door if the project doesn't deliver the new processes on time.

In one case, the project manager told me: "Heads of Department used to send a junior representative to my project meetings. Now they come in person to tell me when we are not keeping our promises – it has become a priority for them".

Note that the improvement being measured is NOT the time released, but a performance improvement in a core activity, achieved as a result of time redeployed.

When I started to use this approach I discovered that just knowing whether a Benefits Realisation Plan had been developed, allowed me to predict how successful a project was likely to be in delivering indirect benefits.

A Benefits Realisation Plan is a clear sign that management is taking responsibility for delivery of the expected benefits. Without this, any benefits, but particularly efficiency savings projected from process improvement or introduction of new systems, need to be discounted.

You can ask two simple questions to test whether the organisation has a robust approach to benefits realisation:

Does the project/programme have a published benefits realisation plan?	YES	NO
Are Dept/Division heads formally accountable for achieving the performance improvements enabled by the project/programme?	YES	NO

Benefits Realisation Outcomes

Yes/Yes (Low risk)	The existence of a formal benefits realisation plan, with clear accountability on the part of operational managers suggests that this project will achieve all the planned process efficiency benefits.
Yes/No (Medium risk)	Having a formal benefits realisation plan means that the project has a chance of delivering the desired efficiency savings, but the improvements will only happen if operational managers are clearly responsible, as user representatives in the project, for adopting the new processes and redeploying released resources to drive increased productivity in their departments. This also creates a healthy 'pull' dynamic for the project. Use existing key service targets to measure improvements rather than trying to monitor time savings.
No/Yes (Medium risk)	Giving operational managers responsibility for making changes happen in their departments means that the project has a good chance of delivering the desired efficiency savings. However, the lack of a formal benefits realisation plan means that they will not be held accountable in practice – put one in place.
No/No (High risk)	Develop a formal benefits realisation plan and ensure that operational managers are made accountable, as user representatives in the project, for adopting the new processes and redeploying released resources to drive increased productivity in their departments. This also creates a healthy 'pull' dynamic for the project. Use existing key service targets to measure improvements rather than trying to monitor time savings.

Here's an example of the difference having a Benefits Realisation Plan made to one organisation:

A university needed to upgrade its ramshackle way of accounting for student attendance. The system, based on a series of spreadsheets built in-house over years was supposed to monitor and control student registration, attendance and degree awards, but the last government audit had identified a number of students who were no longer at the university but were still on the 'payroll' for government funding. The specification for a replacement system was put out to tender and a supplier appointed to bring in a new system. One benefit claimed in the business case that was approved by the Principal and his senate (the university's management board) was that the new system would save enough money to pay for the system over two years.

I was working on another project for the university at the time and was asked by the finance manager to look at the business case. I immediately spotted a flaw: 70% of the savings were projected to come from reducing the workload on administrative staff and increasing their efficiency. When I asked to see the benefits realisation plan, it turned out that nobody had given any real thought to how these savings were to be achieved.

The work that I undertook to identify where the savings would come from – and who should take responsibility for making sure they did – became the blueprint for the approach described in this chapter and which is now an important element in the INPACT toolkit. The monitoring and control work was rationalised and allocated to the Finance Department. Other departments reorganised their staff workloads to release a total of three people who were retrained and are now running the university's alumni activities, vital as the basis for its fundraising campaign.

Section 1 of this book focused on organisational capability. Section 2 looked at the project. This section has covered a number of the elements I have found to be key to the delivery of a successful transformation project. So now you should be ready to carry out an assessment, build the route-map and implement the action plan. Let's do it!

SECTION 4: ASSESSMENT & IMPLEMENTATION

15

Carrying Out an INPACT Assessment

The objective of an INPACT Assessment is to quickly gauge the capability of the organisation and whether they are likely to succeed in getting the planned benefits from the project they are embarking on. A typical assessment consists of the following steps:

1. Map the Organisational Culture and Business Process Capability and combine these into an Organisational Capability indicator.

2. Test for shared objectives, assess the complexity of the project and analyse the gap between your capability and the complexity of your project.

3. Look for other factors that will impact on your success, such as the levels of distrust in your organisation, the lack of a robust Benefits Realisation Plan, lack of influence on external stakeholders or the appropriateness of the IT solution.

4. Calculate the potential impact of these indicators on the business case and share the results with your senior management to gain their ownership of the issues.

5. Develop a Route-Map and implement an Action Plan to overcome the barriers and mitigate the risks.

1. Map your Organisational Capability

Use descriptions in Chapter 3 to identify the predominant organisational culture in your organisation (or that part of the organisation affected by the change project).

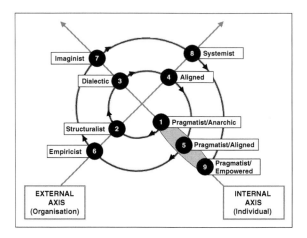

Assess your business process capability maturity using the CMM model in Chapter 4.

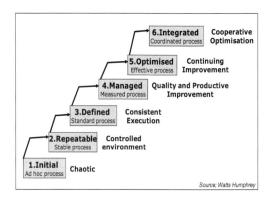

Combine the results as described in Chapter 4 to position your organisation's capability to manage change and take advantage of modernization and transformation projects.

ORGANISATIONAL CAPABILITY

Business Process Capability

Organisational Culture	Level 1	2	3	4	5
1. Pragmatic/ Anarchic	Low	Low			
2. Structuralist	Low	Low	Med		
3. Dialectic	Low	Med	Med	Med	
4. Aligned	Med	Med	Med	High	High
5. Pragmatic/ Aligned			High	High	High
6. Empiricist			High	High	High
7. Imaginist			High	High	V.High
8. Systemist			High	V.High	V.High
9. Pragmatic/Empowered			V.High	V.High	V.High

2. Test for shared objectives, assess the complexity of the project, analyse the capability/complexity gap

Ask the three linked questions of key stakeholders and score the responses:

- In your view, what are the main objectives and benefits of the project?
- Who is responsible for delivering the benefits?
- What are your responsibilities in the project?

A lower than 75% score indicates a lack of consistency in people's perception of the project's objectives that will undermine take-up later in the project.

Now ask the questions of your stakeholders that will allow you to plot the three complexity factors. This establishes where your project lies actually on the scale of 'Simple' to 'Too Complex', as opposed to where people think it lies.

Stakeholders: the number of people involved (an approximation might be those stakeholders represented on steering and project groups)

Processes: the number of business activities and processes that will be affected (for example the number of manual processes an automation project will 'touch' and change)

Time: Expected implementation timescale in months (from issue of spec/ITT to planned completion of roll-out)

Map the results on the exponential complexity scale.

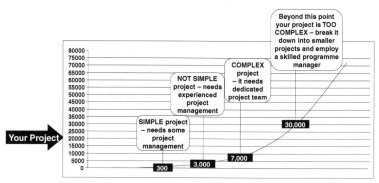

Put the results of the complexity measurement into the context of your organizational capability to show the **relative** complexity of the project.

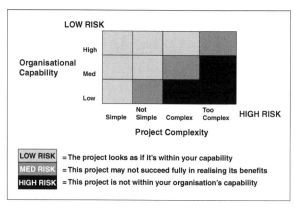

3. Look for other factors that will impact on your success

Distrust: Identify the level of distrust between stakeholder managers, their own managers and staff and map this to show the potential impact of distrust on your project:

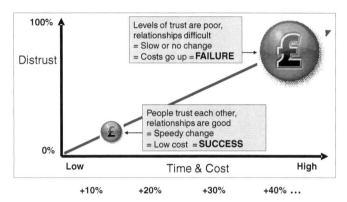

Benefits Realisation: Ask the two questions in Chapter 14 and assess the likelihood that claimed benefits will actually be realised.

Yes/Yes (Low risk)	We would expect this project to achieve the planned process efficiency benefits.
Yes/No or No/Yes (Medium risk)	The desired improvements will only happen if operational managers are given clear responsibility for adopting the new processes and redeploying released resources.
No/No (High risk)	Unless you develop a formal benefits realisation plan and ensure that operational managers are made accountable for adopting the new processes and redeploying released resources, you will not achieve increased productivity from this project.

External stakeholders: The project may involve stakeholders that are outside the project manager's sphere of influence, such as suppliers or partnering organisations. These can have a significant impact on the project. If you suspect that this is the case with your project, include an appropriate weighting when you calculate the potential impact in the next step.

IT solution: Similarly, if your project revolves around the introduction or upgrade of an IT system to drive and support new, more efficient ways of working or give you capabilities to scale up or deliver new services, consider the five key questions in Chapter 13. If they indicate an overall 'Low' score, include an appropriate weighting under that heading in the next step.

4. Calculate the potential impact of these indicators on the business case and share the results

Each of these measures can be used to calculate the potential impact of the barriers on the project's business case. Each will have an impact on either the project's costs and timescales or the levels of savings and revenue benefits, if the underlying causes are not addressed. Plot your findings on the table, giving a weighting % for each based on the indicators and your own knowledge of the more detailed story that lies behind the scores, along the lines shown.

Each indicator will be your assessment of the increased cost and/or timescale, or reduction in revenue benefits, based on the data you have collected, combined with your experience. So these figures *are* subjective, which is why I have called them indicators.

Component	Status	Potential Impact	
		Time/Cost + %	Benefits - %
ORGANISATION CAPABILITY			
Organisational Culture Map	H/M/L		
Business Process Capability Maturity (incl visibility of process)			
PROJECT			
Clarity of objectives	Disparity %		
Complexity of project	Simple/Not Simple/ Complex/Too Complex		
Project Resource Plan	H/M/L		
DELIVERY OF PROJECT			
Trust & Relationships	%		
Benefits Realisation Plan	YY/YN/NN		
Line Resources Plan	H/M/L		
OTHER FACTORS			
Role of external stakeholders	H/M/L		
Robustness of IT Plan	H/M/L		
Total potential impact on project timescales/costs		+ %	
Total potential impact on benefits			-%
Overall impact on ROI – break-even			

As you collect case study evidence of project assessments, you will be able to firm up on these figures, establishing benchmarks against which your assessment can be compared.

I have found that the most effective way to use these indicators is to run a workshop after an assessment, at which the key decision-makers are represented. Bring together senior managers, process users and stakeholders and use the model to open up the dialogue.

That will enable senior managers and stakeholders to recognise the capability limitations of the organisation to manage the proposed changes – and begin to focus on tackling the barriers to success.

Sounds like a Dialectic style approach, doesn't it. That's no accident. It is usually that style that is missing in most projects.

I put up my assessments and ask people to challenge them, which they usually do, energetically! Don't let that put you off. The purpose is to negotiate a compromise figure which is acceptable to the participants and gives them ownership of the issues, but which still allows you to insert something in the column each time. Then do the maths. If you have agreed a set of quantified barriers, the table will demonstrate quite clearly what the impact would be on the business case if nothing is done about them.

And the fact that you have arrived at the figures together, ensures they are 'owned' by everyone around the table.

Notice what this approach is doing – it translates 'soft' issues into language that senior managers understand: figures, impact on ROI... You are shifting the problem across into their model of the world.

If the project was unrealistic but your senior management had not been prepared to accept the fact, you can be confident that this approach will achieve a shift in their mindsets. If you needed more resources to implement the project than was being offered, this should improve your prospects of getting them. And if the problem actually lies in the weakness of the organisation's capability, this should emerge without you pointing any fingers.

5. Develop a Route-Map, implement an Action Plan

You have carried out the assessments, have come up with some findings and have gained senior management buy-in to your conclusions – or at least a watered down version. What now? The next step is clearly to come up with a Route-Map and an Action Plan to deal with the issues that you have uncovered, so that's what the next chapters will deal with – first the Route-Map.

16

Developing a Route-Map to Improve Your Capability for Change

Map Organisational Capability	Develop capability/ complexity indicator	Measure trust, check for BRP & other key factors	Calculate impact on business case, share results	Develop Route Map, implement Action Plan

In most examples that I have come across, it is largely the culture barriers that undermine the project's success, so this chapter provides a Route-Map for you to navigate through the Organisational Culture model and understand what you need to do to push the organisation up the spiral. The stronger the Organisational Culture, the better the organisation will adapt and respond to change.

At each level, I ask two questions:

- *If we are here now, where do we need to be?*
- *What if we don't change?*

The first identifies what needs to change. The second gives you the ammunition you might need to defend the change – it describes the future if you stay where you are.

As you saw in Chapters 2 and 3, each management style in the spiral builds on the earlier ones. Each style is a necessary part of the evolution of the organisation. So, for example, a small company needs to move away from its initial Pragmatic/Anarchic style to a more Structuralist style if it wishes to develop more efficient ways of working and to scale up its operation; a bureaucratic organisation must develop a more Dialectic culture if it wants to get the best out of its people and respond to its customers in a fast-changing world.

162

What if the organisation doesn't take these steps?

Over time, each style degenerates, as people become complacent and useful elements become fixed and difficult to change. So the NHS hospital that has been stuck in a Structuralist management style for some time is finding that silo working and tribalism have now made it very hard to bring in new standardised systems or develop more 'mature' styles such as collaborative working and knowledge-sharing.

Worse still, in this extreme example, every part of the organisation is reverting more and more to a Pragmatic/Anarchic style of working, as the cohesion and corporate identity of the organisation disintegrates and is replaced by local fiefdoms and small groups of self-interested workers, fighting to survive by 'doing their own thing'.

Reorganisation can improve things, but only if it introduces a Dialectic style of management, rather than simply restructuring the organisation. Many of the corporate restructuring exercises during the 90's saw organisations alternating between a centralist structure and a devolved way of working. Note that both of these are simply poles along the EXTERNAL axis. The restructuring did little to improve performance as it did not focus equally on involving people.

It is unlikely that any of the 9 points on the spiral will accurately and completely describe any organisation's management style. The intention is to capture the dominant style in that part of the organisation affected by a change project. If the project is organisation-wide, it can also be used to spot where there are significant differences between parts of the organisation.

Once you have decided which description/s to work with, it is fairly easy to think about how to move to the next level on the spiral. In the following pages, I outline for each stage what you might do to shift a dominant culture and acquire the capabilities of one further up the spiral.

If the purpose of using the Organisational Culture model is to assess the capability of the organisation to cope with a specific change or transformation project, I suggest that the assessment should be carried out first across those parts of the organisation specifically affected by the proposed changes.

Level 1 > 2

Where are we now? Level 1: Pragmatic /Anarchic
Where do we need to be? Level 2: Structuralist

If your dominant style is Level 1: Pragmatic /Anarchic, what do you need to do to move up the organisational culture spiral?

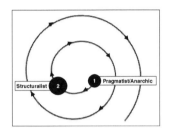

The chances are, you need structure. Build into this corporate structure all the elements required to manage more consistently and more effectively, including: clear policies, roles and responsibilities, documented governance and decision-making processes, accountability for performance, good communications and reporting processes, success measures etc.

Your ability to scale up at low cost (the secret to successful growth) depends on having this structure and the associated culture in place and working smoothly. That may mean bringing in new skills and experience. You will need to pay particular attention to your organisation's business process capability, which I dealt with in Chapter 4.

Remember, like all the organisational cultures, a Structuralist culture is in itself not a bad way to work – it's only what happens when the culture degenerates, that's counter-productive.

What if we don't change?
Your flexibility, response to market changes and speed of decision-making may appear to be good, but these will depend on the time and attention given to them by specific individuals – they won't be consistent. That means that your organisation does not have the capability to grow or become more efficient.

Level 2 > 3

Where are we now? Level 2: Structuralist
Where do we need to be? Level 3: Dialectic

If your dominant style is Level 2: Structuralist, what do you need to do to move up the organisational culture spiral?

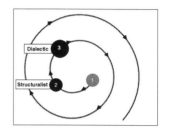

You need to break down the silos and encourage people to share information. However the Structuralist culture is often very strongly entrenched and difficult to change. You need to change the system if you want to change how people behave. It is no good trying to encourage sharing in an environment where targets are driving people to be competitive rather than collaborative. So do develop cross-organisational communication and knowledge-sharing networks. Do use task forces and transformation projects to get people working collaboratively. But do also focus attention on the way the organisation sets targets and rewards performance. If possible, design a better framework and more effective targets, (you could, for example, start with '100% customer satisfaction, first time') and find ways to reward collaborative behaviour. You will also need to pay close attention to the Process side of the change, with an effective information system that works across the internal boundaries, to enable sharing and collaboration.

What if we don't change?
Changing a Stucturalist organisation is a real challenge – I don't want to suggest otherwise, but if you don't, you can expect that the tribalism and silo working will grow, increasingly dominating your organisational culture. Poor communications, distrust and in-fighting will distract from focusing on customer needs, meaning that your top management will not be able to respond in time to changing market requirements. Existing rules and processes will be used to block change, preventing you from taking advantage of new and better ways of working. Your organisation will continue on its downward spiral into stagnation and reduced efficiency.

Level 3 > 4

Where are we now? Level 3: Dialectic
Where do we need to be? Level 4: Aligned

If your dominant style is Level 3: Dialectic, what do you need to do to move up the organisational culture spiral?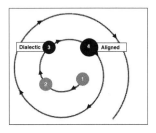
To succeed, a dialectic culture needs strong, inspirational leadership to maintain the vision and a good level of compliance to mandatory policies to ensure that productivity is not sacrificed on the altar of knowledge-sharing. You should be aiming for a situation where at least 75% of people in the organisation understand and are committed to a shared set of corporate values. Involve people in developing and implementing these to make them personal. Involve them also in standardising processes and developing end-to-end performance measures to bring in more efficient ways of working.

Without this the Dialectic culture deteriorates back to a Pragmatic/Anarchic culture, where everyone is allowed to do their own thing and the organisation cannot benefit.

What if we don't change?

Although an organisation with a Dialectic culture has the capability to work together to solve problems, without leadership and compliance to well-managed processes, this capability may become more important than responding quickly and appropriately to changing customer needs. People are encouraged to share information and exchange ideas, so that's what they do. Meetings become talking shops, nobody wants to make a decision and the pace of change slows and stagnates.

Level 4 > 5

Where are we now? Level 4: Aligned

Where do we need to be? Level 5: Pragmatic/Aligned

If your dominant style is Level 4: Aligned, what do you need to do to move up the organisational culture spiral?

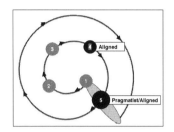

Devolve day-to-day decision-making as far down the organisation and as close to the customer as possible. Exploit the aligned culture and efficient processes to bring in a LEAN approach, stripping out unnecessary checks and multiple levels of authorisation. Introduce initiative rewards, shareholding schemes etc to reward individual performance but remember that the real key to making a Pragmatic/Aligned culture work is the positive relationships between managers and their staff. Focus particularly on building the Pragmatic/Aligned culture at this work-group level.

What if we don't change?

You will not be taking full advantage of the strengths you have developed. In time, good staff will get disillusioned and leave, putting pressure on resources and diluting your capacity to respond to change.

Level 5 > 6

Where are we now? Level 5: Pragmatic/Aligned
Where do we need to be? Level 6: Empiricist

If your dominant style is Level 5: Pragmatic/Aligned, what do you need to do to move up the organisational culture spiral?

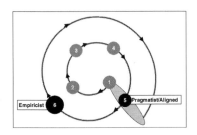

Develop a knowledge management strategy that builds on your strengths. Encourage people to access information and ideas from outside the organisation. Introduce horizon-scanning and benchmarking. Bring your customers and suppliers into your design, planning and delivery processes. Collaborate. Bring in systems that enable you to combine structured and unstructured data from external as well as internal sources to improve the accuracy and timeliness of decision-making. Managers who are well-informed can be sensitive to changes in the external environment as they are happening, not when they are history. They can assess risk faster and better and respond more appropriately, with decisions based on timely, accurate facts.

What if we don't change?

If you fail to exploit your strengths in accessing, internalising and exploiting 'real-world' data to improve the speed, reach and accuracy of decision-making, you cannot be a top-performing organisation. The combination of devolved decision-making and an overdependence on internally-generated information could even take you back to some of the negative features of Pragmatic/ Anarchic and Structuralist styles. Failure to reach out to customers and suppliers will hinder your ability to recognise and to respond appropriately to changing requirements.

168

Level 6 > 7

Where are we now? Level 6: Empiricist
Where do we need to be? Level 7: Imaginist

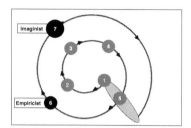

If your dominant style is Level 6: Empiricist, what do you need to do to move up the organisational culture spiral?

You have a high quality of information flow and a devolved, fully aligned style of decision-making. That means that your managers can focus on more strategic issues. Are they doing so? It may be that your organisation does not have the right calibre of manager at this level. It may also be that you have not embraced innovation and creativity as forces for change. You managers may not feel able to set aside the 'space' in their day for thinking time to digest the information, or to take advantage of opportunities to encounter new ideas. You need to develop or acquire managers who will be able to use the high quality of information available and ensure that they have the right environment to make intuitive, forward-looking decisions. Finally, the Board has to trust these decisions and act on them for this culture to have its full impact on performance. Of all the steps in the organisational culture spiral, this is probably the most challenging.

What if we don't change?
Unless you take this step and ensure that you have the right calibre of managers to lead the change, your focus will remain tactical rather than strategic and there will be a tendency to revert to the short-term, interventionist style of management that is a feature of less mature organisations. Your organisation will show the negative features of an Empiricist culture: information being collected and stored mechanically, rather than as usable knowledge; an emphasis on quantity rather than on quality of information; managers drowning in paper; a rise in duplicated databases and systems and a reversion to a silo-based Structuralist culture.

Level 7 > 8

Where are we now? Level 7: Imaginist
Where do we need to be? Level 8: Systemist

If your dominant style is Level 7: Imaginist, what do you need to do to move up the organisational culture spiral?

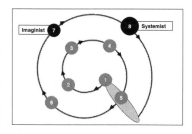

The evolution of an Imaginist management style should have given the CEO and the Board the time and the information they need to understand the organisation in its various contexts (shareholders, customers, employees, local community, technical, wider economic and ecological contexts) and lead it in the right direction, spearheading change and transformation programmes designed to encourage innovation and equip the organisation for the challenges that are appearing on the longer-term horizon. This is a vital step in the organisation's culture evolution and requires a special calibre of leader.

What if we don't change?
If top management do not back off and devolve day-to-day operations and short-term running of the organisation to their management team, they will lose the good quality managers very quickly. An inability to refocus Board attention to the longer-term future of the organisation will inevitably lead to a decline in the organisation's performance.

Level 8 > 9

Where are we now? Level 8: Systemist
Where do we need to be? Level 9: Pragmatic/Empowered

If your dominant style is Level 8: Systemist, what do you need to do to move up the organisational culture spiral?

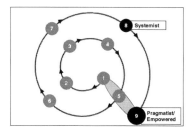

One of the benefits of a well-managed organisation is that it can put more and more responsibility on to the shoulders of its staff. In a Systemist culture, the workforce should be capable of taking on more responsibility for 'going the extra mile' to satisfy their customers. Staff should be encouraged to organise their own work, built on best practice acquired through knowledge-sharing and benchmarking. Time should be allocated to allow people to pursue ideas and collaborate. Innovation and creativity should be recognised as the key assets they are and duly rewarded.

What if we don't change?
A Systemist culture can degenerate as quickly and easily as any other – perhaps more so. There is continuous pressure on your ability to maintain your performance at this level. As people come and go, external conditions change and organisations restructure and refocus, elements of less mature management styles can creep back in. So vigilance is required. Pay attention to supporting and reinforcing the best practices you have developed, through continuous improvement programmes. Complacency is the enemy here. There may be a tendency to apply systems thinking without the necessary sensitivity to local objectives, values and styles of management. If attention is not paid to continually reinforcing the organisational culture, it is inevitable that some degradation will occur. This will lead to lower creativity and a drop in performance.

Level 9

Where are we now? Level 9: Pragmatic /Empowered

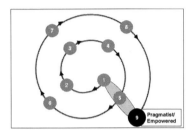

If your dominant style is Level 9: Pragmatic/Empowered, it would appear that there is nothing more you need to do – you have reached the goal – the final step in the organisational culture spiral.

However, it is rare to find an organisation that has really achieved this high level of cultural maturity homogeneously across the whole organisation, so the focus should be to bring the rest of the organisation up to the same standard.

What if we don't change?

You have come full circle from Pragmatic/Anarchic, through Pragmatic/Aligned, to Pragmatic/Empowered.

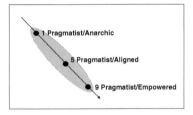

Failure to take this final step and support full empowerment of staff to run their own operation will mean that you will lose some of your best people and your organisation will not be able to take advantage of the creativity and energy that this way of working can release. Inevitably this will take your organisation backwards – in the worst case, potentially all the way back to Pragmatic/Anarchic. A truly Pragmatic/ Empowered culture is a sophisticated social system that is not well-understood by outsiders. The arrival of a new CEO or the involvement of outside consultants can be fatally disruptive. What takes years to develop can take months to dismantle.

I hope this chapter has provided a useful route-map to enable you to identify what needs to change in order for the organisation's culture to shift. Now let's look at how to build an action plan to bring all this together and make change happen.

17

Overcoming the Barriers to Success: The Action Plan

Map Organisational Capability	Develop capability/ complexity indicator	Measure trust, check for BRP & other key factors	Calculate impact on business case, share results	Develop Route Map, implement Action Plan

This chapter focuses on what to do about the barriers to success you have uncovered. Some of these may be deep-seated cultural or process capability barriers that might need a significant amount of time and effort to shift – others may be simpler, like getting greater clarity of objectives or implementing a Benefits Realisation Plan.

I cannot predict all the issues and barriers that you will uncover, nor could I propose solutions in detail to deal with them in this book, but what follows is a guide to the key implications if the status of the assessment component is high risk e.g. the complexity of the project is HIGH relative to the capability of your organisation. It should give you a clear approach that you can adapt to your own assessment and Action Plan. Although I have concentrated on the worst case scenarios here, you can obviously apply the same framework to medium risk results.

I look first at the Organisation, then the Project and finally at External Stakeholders, one of the factors that often impacts on change projects. I use the 'traffic light' indicators to highlight the high/medium/low risk results – don't forget, the purpose of the Action Plan is to get board level sign-off on key work that needs to be done before, during and after the project is implemented, so make it easy for them to focus on the important stuff!.

ORGANISATION

Component	Implication	Action required if Status = HIGH RISK
Organisational Culture	The lack of information-sharing, alignment and empowerment will jeopardise the success of the project. At the very least it will mean poor take-up and a lower than planned level of benefits.	A programme of interaction and dialogue across the organisation is urgently needed to improve the organisational culture. This needs to include increasing trust, see below.
Business Process Capability	The organisation's business process capability is poor. This means that any projects which seek to standardise and improve processes to achieve greater efficiency will be very difficult to achieve.	Consider carrying out a programme to raise the levels of business process capability ahead of implementing the project or using the project itself to inject the necessary disciplines. In this case it is crucial for the Board to make compliance to the new processes mandatory.
Trust	The high levels of distrust will slow down and may even stop the project.	Distrust and lack of respect between managers and staff and between departments needs to be investigated and tackled as an urgent priority. The project itself could be used to raise the level of trust and make people feel that they count, if planned and implemented with the involvement of these stakeholders.

PROJECT		
Component	**Implication**	**Action required if Status = HIGH RISK**
Clarity of objectives	A lack of shared understanding of the project's objectives will reduce its priority and may prejudice the chances of success. Correcting this once the project has kicked off requires a significant effort, delaying roll-out and adding to costs.	Formal consultation has been insufficient – further consultation and dialogue is required with all stakeholders. Creation of a user panel is strongly recommended to share responsibility for delivery – see Benefits Realisation, below.
Complexity of project	The project is too complex to manage in the context of the organisation's capability and as it is currently planned and resourced. It may have to be broken down into several projects and the roll-out timescale may have to be extended. This could increase project timescales and delay realisation of benefits, with an impact on ROI.	Implementation should be re-planned in phases over a longer timescale and benefit realisation brought in line. A full-time programme manager may be needed, in addition to sufficient resources allocated in departments. Unless these resources can be found in-house, they should be brought in using external experience and skills to accelerate the pace of the project. The earlier realisation of savings should pay for the additional costs.
Benefits Realisation	Modernisation of processes can deliver significant efficiencies, but these will not achieve savings unless managers are targeted with redeploying released resources in their department. Unless this is tackled, discount any indirect savings in the business case.	Operational managers need to be made accountable, as user representatives in the project, for adopting the new processes to drive increased productivity in their departments. Use existing key service targets to measure improvements rather than trying to monitor time savings.

175

External Stakeholders		
Component	**Implication**	**Action required if Status = HIGH RISK**
External Factors: Relationship with key stakeholders	There is not the foundation of trust needed to engage external stakeholders (collaborators, partners, key suppliers, etc.) and get their co-operation to make the necessary changes. The impact of this on project timescales can be significant and the project may not succeed.	An energetic and persuasive consultation and communication programme is needed to ensure that external stakeholders are ready and able to accept their role in the planned changes. This attention needs to continue as the system is rolled out, to ensure take-up and compliance. If you suspect that this will not deliver the desired cooperation, do not ignore it – you need to modify your plans, extending timescales, reducing the ambition of the project or finding alternative partners.
External Factors: Selecting the IT solution	If the technology lies at the heart of the project, driving and/or supporting change, any shortfall in the way it was specified or is being implemented will cripple the project	Use the 5 questions in Chapter 13 to test whether you have a problem. If so, focus on dealing with that before proceeding any further – it's that important.

The Action Plan will help you to prioritise where to put the effort to improve the success rates of your change projects. Some of this will need to be done in preparation for the project, some will take longer than the project implementation lifecycle. Change management is like that!

Okay, that is as far as I can take you on this journey...for the moment. Apart from some case studies in the Appendices, we've arrived. I plan to continue to refine the models and tools in the next year with the help of Westminster Business School. They have kindly given me access to their Executive MBA Programme students to enable me to build up a database of evidence to support and calibrate the models and tools.

Thank you for travelling with me and allowing me to tell you about my ideas and insights. I hope you weren't too bored or infuriated – the fact that you have read to the end suggests that we are still on speaking terms at least (!) and that you have found something you can take away from the book that will change mindsets and make a real difference to a project that needs to succeed.

Do please send me your own assessment results and any suggestions for improving the assessment methodology. I'd also like to hear about successful change project stories or insights you had after reading this book.

I'm at: peterd@imaginist.co.uk.

Good luck!

Appendix A
e-Procurement in a Local Authority

Here is a fully worked case study based on an assessment carried out in a Local Authority. Some of the details have been omitted for confidentiality reasons.

1. Introduction

The client is a Local Authority with 5,500 employees. The e-Procurement Strategic Review was undertaken ahead of a project planned to bring in an electronic marketplace and modernise the purchase-to-pay (P2P) processes, most of which are still carried out manually at present.

Some 1,000 managers and staff and around 7,500 suppliers are thought to be involved in purchasing, invoice processing and payment for goods and services – a spend of £200m last year.

The objective is to roll out e-procurement within 6 months. The Executive Board had identified a number of potential risks in the early planning of the project and the review was commissioned to bring these into focus, assess their importance and develop strategies to deal with them.

They included:

- A failure of a previous process improvement exercise to deliver expected results
- The issue of compliance in a highly devolved organisation
- The significant levels of change over the past 2-3 years, resulting in 'change fatigue'
- The lack of strategic priority afforded to procurement by department heads and operational managers.

2. Approach

Imaginist carried out a review of:

1. The project
2. The organisation
3. External factors, such as the relationship with key suppliers.

The review followed the INPACT assessment methodology, which focuses on both process and culture transformation, identifying the main barriers to success and recommending prioritised actions to address these.

3. Results

The review identified that the lack of attention to both process and culture issues would prejudice the realisation of the planned e-procurement project benefits.

A calculation of the impact of the underlying barriers was presented to the client, together with the reasons for this conclusion.

After discussion it was accepted that the project could take twice as long to implement as planned (and cost 70% more) and that the return in efficiency and cost savings may be as much as 80% below expected levels. The reasoning and basis for this conclusion are detailed in the remainder of the report. The impact assessment calculation is summarised at the end of the report.

A programme of work to deal with the underlying barriers was put in place, in line with the Action Plan and the e-procurement project roll-out plan was revised to allow for the greater complexity revealed by the review.[21]

---

[21] Note that this assessment was tailored to the client's requirements; some headings vary from the standard methodology laid out in Chapter 15.

4. The assessment

Organisation

The culture of an organisation and the way it manages its processes are key to assessing how well it will respond to change. The Organisational Culture model is used to indicate the prevalent culture and the Process Management Capability Maturity model is used to assess the way the organisation manages its processes. From these analyses, an indication can be developed of the organisation's capability to manage the changes.

Other indicators are then used to measure the potential for success of the project, including the level of distrust across the organisation and the robustness of the benefits realisation plan.

Using the INPACT Organisational Capability tool, the management culture of the organisation was found to be a mix of Pragmatist (1) and Structuralist (2).

Within departments, there was evidence of a degree of pragmatism (1) at managerial level, but this almost disappeared below managerial level, with staff reluctant to act unless instructed to do so.

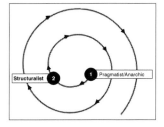

The well-defined structuralist (2) culture worked quite well but with a strong tendency towards bureaucracy and 'tribalism'. In this Structuralist culture, managers and staff often hide behind the rules and use them as reasons not to take the initiative. Change is seen as largely negative, disruptive and to be avoided. Communication is channelled up and down the management structure of the organisation, with little real dialogue between staff and managers in different departments. In this 'tribal' culture, there is little sharing of ideas and knowledge across the organisation, including within the senior management team.

There was no clear alignment between individuals' aspirations and the organisation's policies and strategic direction, which meant that when changes were introduced, they tended to be imposed and resented. In fact most interviewees, at all levels, felt overloaded and under-resourced, not really coping with their day-to-day workload and suffering the effects of several generations of process change (each leaving unofficial and ad hoc work-arounds in their wake).

Although they recognised the need for cost savings, they could not see how staffing levels could be reduced any further and still enable them to carry out the jobs they wanted to do. Despite the continual pressures there was still a level of commitment and concern for the effect of this on the public, their 'clients'. There was also a level of frustration that nobody was asking them what would work best.

This lack of empowerment at the staff level also flowed through into the way managers made decisions – the process is slow and convoluted and is informed by poor management information, which results in high level policy never fully translating into action and short-term decisions being taken, rather than well-informed, far-reaching and creative decisions. Senior managers in this environment are necessarily more interventionist than systemist (being able to steer from behind and take the longer-term view).

The level of trust between managers and their staff was found to be fairly good. There was less trust in the relationships between the managers and the Senior Management Team, but that is not unusual. However the levels of trust between departments was worryingly low – distrust and lack of respect coloured almost all the relationships. Cross-departmental communication and knowledge sharing was constrained by this distrust and the implication of this situation is that the take-up of e-procurement is likely to fall into the same patterns.

The degree to which managers and staff 'own' the planned changes correlates well to the amount of effort they are prepared to put into making the changes happen and how well the project will generate the expected improvements. The review did not find any real ownership of the proposed changes in the affected departments – and this included some Heads of Department, which is worrying. Managers with little direct interest in procurement will not give the project sufficient priority and their staff will not adopt the new processes, preferring to carry on as before.

The concern among some managers is that the project will not achieve the desired results but the organisation will have moved on to the next change project and nothing will be done to improve performance until budget constraints force another effort to move to the more efficient processes.

Capability Maturity: on the Capability Maturity Model (CMM) scale, the organisation is functioning at mostly level 2 (Controlled environment; repeatable, stable processes), with elements of level 1 (Chaotic; ad hoc processes) and some areas at level 3 (Consistent Execution; defined, standard processes).

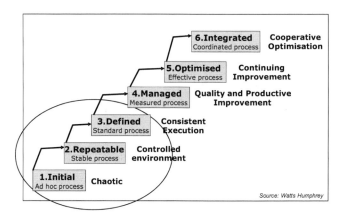

There is no evidence of properly managed or measured processes (Level 4) although that is the level of maturity the organisation claims for itself and that is the level of capability the project under review requires. There is therefore a significant risk that it will not succeed without significant changes in the way processes are managed across the organisation.

One significant aspect of the immaturity of the organisation is the lack of commitment from CEO and Board level through to operational managers to making the project a success. Compliance to the new automated procurement processes needs to be mandatory and unless this is accepted by everyone involved in the changes, this project is destined not to achieve its goals.

182

As would be expected in a predominantly CMM level 2 organisation, visibility of existing process is poor – there has been little real process analysis done at a sufficiently detailed level to understand the implications of the automation of the P2P processes.

It is likely that quite a lot of the existing procurement processes will still need to be undertaken manually, at least in part, and particularly in complex service areas such as Social Services. Unless this is addressed and decisions taken on how to manage the parallel use of manual and automated processes, the tendency will be for managers and staff to ignore the new automated processes, undermining its roll-out.

The Project

The project was assessed for clarity of objectives, complexity, robustness of its resource plan and how benefits were planned to be realised.

Clarity of objectives: the research identified a worrying lack of consistency in the perception of the objectives of the project on the part of key stakeholders across the organisation. Although there had been formal consultation, most managers and staff had little interest in the project, only a vague idea of what was going to happen and no real commitment to their part in realising the intended benefits. There was general fear that it would mean a loss of control and jobs.

Complexity of project: The project was assessed using the INPACT Exponential Complexity Equation and came out with a score putting it in the 'Highly Complex Project' bracket. This had not been anticipated by participants who had assumed it was no higher than 'Complex'. The advice for projects in the 'Highly Complex' bracket is: "Beyond this point your project is too complex – break it down into separate projects and employ a programme manager."

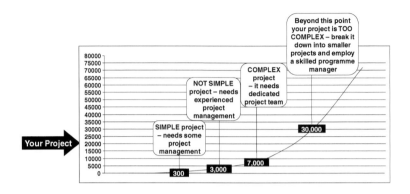

Highly complex projects require full-time experienced programme management and dedicated implementation resources, neither of which were being allocated to this project – see below. They are unlikely to be fully successful in an immature organisation i.e. lower than CMM level 3, without injecting greater discipline and control over the way the organisation manages its processes.

Robustness of Resource Plan: The project was to be rolled out by a project board led by the procurement manager with support from the IT department and the organisation's Business Transformation Manager (who was also rolling out a CRM system). There were no plans to allocate a full-time experienced project manager to the project or to dedicate department resources to implementation – in fact none of the project board were being allocated to work full-time on the project. These resources are clearly inadequate for a project of this complexity.

Benefits realisation: There was no benefits realisation plan, despite quite substantial claims for cost savings and efficiency improvement as a result of the modernisation of procurement. No benchmarking had been carried out to ascertain actual costs of the manual processes, relying on national published figures for the business plan.

Automation and streamlining of P2P processes can lead to substantial time savings, but only in small increments, across a large number of staff. Tracking this is almost impossible, but it is possible to task managers to redeploy this released time on to other

184

operationally key areas which are already subject to monthly or quarterly performance targets – and track the improvement in these. This creates a healthy 'pull' dynamic for the project.

The review found that Heads of Department and service heads were resigned to cuts in budget to reflect the savings available when the e-procurement system was implemented, but they were not being held directly accountable for achieving or reporting efficiency benefits and there were no plans to involve them in measuring improvements. Without this involvement, efficiency benefits will not be realised in practice.

Apart from improved process efficiency, the other two main areas of benefit from automating and streamlining P2P processes are:

- price savings from the wider use of framework contracts and online catalogues
- back office staff reductions from the simplification of invoice handling.

Price savings depend on a sound analysis of spend and use of suppliers, followed by dedicated effort to improving procurement performance. None of this had been done in preparation for the e-procurement roll-out and did not seem to be in the project plan. Framework contracts were in place for a few commodity areas but were not being widely used. The procurement manager was waiting for the e-Marketplace to be rolled out to give him the basis to start improving this position. The problem with that was that it put the realisation of price benefits at least 18 months to 2 years out. The procurement manager had not been allocated an increase in the number of staff, nor did he have the skills in his existing team required to achieve these results.

Back office staff reductions depend on two key actions, neither of which appeared in the project plan:

- Simplification of the invoice matching process where reliance can be put on 100% approval of purchase at the ordering stage, i.e. mandatory take-up of online purchase ordering, so nothing gets paid unless it has a PO number.

- Working with suppliers to ensure they are able to accommodate e-invoicing (which most can't) or adoption of a range of approaches such as an 'order flip' capability on the e-Marketplace, Government Purchase cards and 'self-billing'.

The lack of forward planning of these aspects of benefits realisation puts in doubt the ability of the project to achieve the savings set out in the business case.

External stakeholders
From scrutiny of the organisation's spend profile, there would appear to be considerable scope for improvement in the cost effectiveness of its procurement but this needs access to good management information (which the current manual process does not provide) and the cooperation of suppliers, who have to make the changes necessary at their end for e-ordering and e-invoicing to be possible.

Supplier relationship: The organisation has little knowledge of its suppliers, lacks a coherent supplier strategy, does not monitor supplier performance and makes no attempt to develop good, managed supplier relationships with key suppliers.

Less than 20% of the organisation's spend on goods and services is contracted – and where contracts are in place, they are not actively managed for best value. There are a few instances of collaborative procurement with other public sector organisations and some use of framework contracts, including nationally negotiated government contracts but these are not part of a systematic strategy.

Where there is greater attention to supplier performance, in some specialist areas, the focus is on operational delivery of service, rather than value for money and continuous improvement.

This does not bode well for a relatively rapid move to e-ordering and e-invoicing.

What needs to be done to deal with these barriers to success?

The Action Plan table overleaf summarises the status of the assessment elements, draws out the implications for the project (including an indication of the impact on costs and timescales and reduction in levels of benefits if the underlying causes are not addressed) and suggests actions that might be taken to deal with these.

The impact calculations are summarised after the Action Plan. These are not empirically researched figures – they are a consensus view based on experience and discussion with the client, which ensures client ownership of the assessment and the actions needed to avoid the risks indicated.

Note: Many of the barriers impact on both costs and benefits: they typically act both to delay the project (increasing costs and delaying revenue benefits) and reduce take-up and the levels of benefit realised. For the purposes of this assessment, impact is allocated either to costs or benefits, where experience shows there to be the greater impact.

Action Plan: The Organisation

	Component/ Status	Implication	Action required
1	Management Culture L: (Pragmatist)/ (Structuralist)	The lack of alignment and empowerment will reduce the level of benefits from this (and any other change projects) by at least 10%.	A1: A programme of interaction and dialogue across the organisation is urgently needed to improve the management culture. This needs to include increasing top management visibility – see 4: Distrust Factor, below.
2	Capability Maturity L: (Mostly level 2, with elements of level 1 and some areas at level 3)	The project needs a level of organisational maturity which was not evidenced in the strategic review. Experience shows that this is a critical factor and impacts both on time/costs and benefit realisation. The latter is included here – a drop of at least 20%, maybe much more.	A2. It is crucial for the Board to make take-up and compliance to the new processes mandatory. The resources allocated are also not sufficient – discussed in A7, below. The project itself could be used to raise the level of capability maturity, if planned and implemented with a greater involvement of stakeholders, see A3, below.
3	Visibility of process L: (Poor)	The new system will not impact on all procurement, so staff will continue to work with manual processes, particularly in complex service areas. This will reduce the value of the new automated system, undermining its roll-out. The consequential lack of ownership of the changes has been shown to add over 20% to project costs and timescales – and in some cases it has effectively led to the demise of the project.	A3. A process mapping exercise is required to identify those areas where the new e-Marketplace and P2P system will not replace existing processes. Decisions are then needed on how to deal with these to optimise efficiency (including: 'stop doing it unless it adds value' – LEAN). The involvement of system users in the mapping and redesign of processes has the benefit of embedding the principles of process improvement and capability maturity.

4	Trust factor L: (Low across departments)	The low levels of trust will slow down communication and response to calls for action – it may even stop the project. At the very least they will increase costs and timescales by at least 20%.	A4. Distrust and lack of respect for managers and other departments needs to be investigated and tackled as an urgent priority. It often has its roots in poor cross-organisational communication and the lack of top management visibility, which can be addressed as part of a programme of interaction – see A1 above.

Action Plan: The Project

	Component/ Status	Implication	Action required
5	Clarity of objectives L: (Poor)	A lack of shared understanding of the project's objectives reduces its priority and may prejudice the chances of success. Correcting this once the project has kicked off requires a significant effort, delaying roll-out and adding up to 10% to costs.	A5. Formal consultation has been insufficient – further consultation and dialogue is required with all stakeholders. Creation of a user panel is strongly recommended to share responsibility for delivery – see 8: Benefits Realisation, below
6	Complexity of project H: (Too complex)	The project is too complex to manage as it is currently planned and resourced. It will have to be broken down into a phased roll-out – the 6 month timescale is certainly unrealistic. The extended roll-out will increase project costs (see 7, below) and delay realisation of benefits, with an impact of 50% on year 1 revenues. 30% has already been included under 1 and 2, leaving a net 20% incremental impact	A6. Implementation should be re-planned in phases over a longer timescale and benefit realisation brought in line. The difficulty of introducing e-procurement across a number of buyers and suppliers is best dealt with by identifying and rolling out the priority spend categories first.
7	Robustness of resource plan L: (Inadequate)	The lack of full-time project management, together with the lack of top management commitment, strongly indicates a project that will not deliver the expected results. Adding the necessary resource would raise costs by 20% at external consultancy rates but may ensure the project's success.	A7. A full-time project manager is needed, in addition to additional procurement resources and skills to tackle supplier as well as buyer take-up. Unless these resources can be found in-house, they should be brought in using external experience and skills to accelerate the pace of the project. The earlier realisation of savings should pay for the additional costs.

| 8 | Benefits Realisation

L: (No plan) | A significant proportion of the expected benefits from a modernisation project come from efficiency savings that are only achieved if managers redeploy released resources in their department. 40% of the project's cashable savings in year 1 was from process improvement. Given the lack of benefits realisation planning, the authority will be lucky to realise half of this. | A8. Operational managers need to be made accountable, as user representatives in the project, for adopting the new processes and redeploying staff to release resources and drive increased productivity in their departments. Use existing key service targets to measure improvements, rather than trying to monitor time savings. |
| 9 | Relationship with suppliers

L: (Poor) | The lack of knowledge about the supplier base and lack of contract performance management means that there is not the foundation of trust needed to engage suppliers and get their co-operation to make the necessary changes. The impact of this on project timescales can be significant – but even more critically, streamlining of invoicing reduces Accounts Payable headcount, which can make up a third of the potential gains from e-procurement. Although this only comprised 20% of projected revenue savings in year 1, we would not expect to see more than half of this being realised, and that will come from budget cuts than as a result of the project. | A9. A rationalisation of the supply base needs to be carried out before implementation of the e-Marketplace to avoid having to load 7,500 suppliers' details and to take advantage of suppliers already on the e-Marketplace. This requires an analysis and cleansing of the supplier database, which should be carried out by an external service provider to ensure that key data is appended (e.g. impact on local suppliers).

A10. A communication programme is then needed to ensure that all the key suppliers are ready and able to accept e-orders and, where possible, issue e-invoices.

A11. Finally, a supplier adoption plan needs to be put in place to bring key suppliers on board as the system is rolled out to buyers.

A12. It is strongly recommended that an e-contract management system is brought in to improve contract management and supplier performance. |

Impact Assessment Summary Table

Component	Status	Potential Impact	
		Time/Cost + %	Benefits - %
ORGANISATION			
Management Culture Map	L (Pragmatist/Structuralist)		
Business Process Capability Maturity (incl visibility of process)	L (Mostly level 2 with elements of level 1, some areas at level 3)		
Overall Capability Impact estimated at:	L		-20%
PROJECT			
Clarity of objectives	50% (Poor)		
Complexity of project	H (Too Complex)		
Overall Project Impact estimated at:		+20%	
DELIVERY OF PROJECT			
Visibility of process	L (Poor)		
Trust & Relationships	Distrust: H (High throughout organization)		
Benefits Realisation Plan	N/N (no plan)		
Delivery of Project Impact estimated at:		+50%	-10%
OTHER FACTORS			
Role of external stakeholders	L (No supplier relationship management)		
Robustness of IT Plan	M (Known solution, medium risk)		
Other Factors Impact estimated at:			-10%
Total potential impact on project timescales/costs		+70%	
Total potential impact on benefits			-40%

Appendix B
Four Short Case Studies

Here are four of the case studies I have used in the book, pulled together and in full, for easy reference.

Case Study 1. Process Standardisation in an NHS Trust Hospital
Case Study 2. Efficiency Project Recovery in a Central Government Department
Case Study 3. Merger of 2 Private Sector Companies
Case Study 4. Collaboration – Social Housing Organisations

Case study 1: Process Standardisation in an NHS Trust Hospital

An NHS Hospital Trust needed to make significant savings in order to balance its books. One opportunity was to reduce the cost of the £60m-worth of medical supplies it purchased each year. Traditionally these had been ordered by consultants, managers and nursing staff across the hospital, as well as by a central procurement department, but with little central control and no corporate knowledge of the total commitment until the accounts department paid the bills, so:

- no opportunity to leverage the total value of expenditure
- no standardisation on selected best value suppliers
- too little visibility of ordering to manage budgets smoothly and avoid overspend

An e-procurement system had been introduced, but uptake was very slow and patchy.

All attempts to introduce standardised products had foundered on the complete lack of trust between procurement and the clinical managers and consultants.

AN INPACT assessment confirmed that lack of trust across the hospital was almost non-existent and certainly would block all initiatives, even though there was general agreement that something had to be done to reduce costs.

The organisational culture was a mix of Pragmatic/Anarchic and Structuralist: a strong 'command and control' culture prevailed, but within this managers were able to set up their own systems and manage processes in their own way, as long as they achieve clinical standards and performance targets. There were laid-down procedures, but they were only followed if managers saw benefits for themselves and their patients. Process capability was a mix of level 1 (ad hoc) and level 2 (defined).

The analysis indicated that conventional strategies for developing standardised processes would not work here. Instead the strong silo culture had to be accommodated. Standardisation of medical supplies is regarded by NHS as a key part of its drive to improve patient safety, so the recommended strategy was to refocus the standardisation initiative away from cost reduction, onto clinical performance improvement.

The solution was to set up a standardisation panel, championed by the CEO, led by the Head of Finance and the Safety Improvement Manager, populated entirely by clinical managers and consultants, with procurement doing the work *in the background* to identify best value products for trial and putting contracts in place.

In parallel, it was recommended that the e-procurement system be enhanced to provide real-time information to clinical managers so they could use it to manage their budgets. This would help them to gain the confidence to move all ordering over to the electronic system, which would in turn provide better commitment information to management.

Case Study 2: Efficiency Project Recovery in a Central Government Department

An IT system brought into a central government department was supposed to have delivered efficiency benefits that could be translated into performance improvement and budget savings. The trouble was…it hadn't done so.

The IT system was introduced to automate some of the processes carried out by the department to collect and analyse data, for inclusion in a regular report. The idea was to streamline the work, reduce delays in issuing the reports and reduce the headcount by two people. In practice, the system seemed to require more time and effort and none of the benefits were being realised.

An INPACT assessment found that the department was working in a mix of Pragmatic/Anarchic and Structuralist organisational cultures.

Managers were largely focused on meeting the plethora of targets by which the department's performance was measured and had developed their own, fairly efficient ways of working to achieve these targets. Their teams were not sharing information efficiently and gave little priority to getting the report out on time if that conflicted with more urgent work.

Process capability was mostly a mix of level 1 (ad hoc process) and level 2 (defined process) with some cross-department systems, such as finance, at level 3 (repeatable processes). There was little visibility of end-to-end processes and where new systems like the IT system were introduced (with little consultation), they impacted piecemeal on the workload of individual members of staff.

The assessment identified that there had been no consultation when the IT system was introduced, so the level of local buy-in was nil. The system was not very easy to use, training had been inadequate and much of the work was still being done manually. Resistance was therefore high – and heightened further by the silo working and low levels of trust in the department.

No formal benefits realisation plan had been put in place and local managers had not accepted accountability for realising the headcount savings.

A recovery plan was developed to remedy these failings, which succeeded in realising the planned benefits. More importantly it helped the department to recognise the underlying problems and to put in place strategies to build up their organisational capability.

Case Study 3: Merger of Two Private Sector Companies

A small but fast-growing and innovative company has been acquired by a larger organisation. Both are experiencing real problems adapting and accommodating the culture and processes of the other. Using INPACT, the underlying reasons for these difficulties are clarified and it is possible to work out what they need to do to realise the benefits promised by the merger.

The larger company has a strong Structuralist culture. Rules and procedures govern how the organisation works. This has allowed the organisation to become over-bureaucratic, with 'silo working' hindering the sharing of ideas and knowledge across the organisation. Change is slow and decisions are often passed down, with formal but inadequate consultation. The company recently underwent a restructuring and introduced standardised processes and systems across all departments, but these have not yet been fully rolled out and managers and staff are not enthusiastic about yet another change, although they recognise the opportunity this merger represents.

In the smaller company, it's results that count. Management rewards success, so individual members of the team are left to do more or less what they like, as long as they achieve results. So the dominant culture in this company was Pragmatist/Anarchic. There are some laid-down procedures, but people only follow them when it suits them.

New initiatives are adopted only if people see clear benefits for themselves and their performance in doing so.

There are some core systems but information is held and

exchanged quite informally. Managers and staff were told about the merger, not consulted, and some people have already left rather than work in the larger company.

This is a classic situation where the cultures and capabilities of the two organisations are incompatible and where, unless remedial steps are taken quite quickly, the opportunity will evaporate for them to create something greater than the sum of its parts.

Initial work will include:

- Get clarity of objectives for the new combined organisation. This will start by addressing what the customers want and ensuring that this intelligence is widely shared and acted upon.

- Set up cross-department meetings and joint projects to build trust across the new team. This dialectic style needs to be incorporated into the way the new organisation works – and rapidly, or the rot will set in. Reinforce it with an internal directory and regular cross-enterprise briefing sessions as well as encouraging a social network to emerge.

- Analyse existing processes to make them visible, involving and engaging people in both groups to come up with new and efficient processes that capitalise on the positives from both companies. This will not only ensure compliance to the new processes, it will sow the seeds for the new, productive relationships that will underpin the next chapter in the company's development.

- Create a transformation programme, led by the CEO and visibly supported by senior managers, to capture and implement the changes needed to focus the new company and get it working effectively. The larger company will need to change as much and as quickly as the newly acquired company if it wants to acquire the smaller company's ability to grow and innovate. The programme must have a formal benefits realisation plan with operational targets for all managers.

Case Study 4: Collaboration – Social Housing Organisations

A social housing organisation (a not-for-profit 'company' set up to take over the management of housing stock from a council) was being tasked by government to develop collaborative working with seven other social housing organisations in their area, in order to share costs, leverage buying power and raise the quality of housing management. The CEO was concerned that the other organisations had different styles of management and might have lower levels of capability.

The INPACT assessment confirmed that the company ("Company A") had an Organisational Culture that was predominantly Pragmatic/Aligned, moving towards Empiricist. 'Pragmatic/Aligned' means that the way the organisation is managed had achieved a close alignment of the needs and aspirations of the staff with those of the organisation. 'Empiricist' means that information about the outside world (in this case, the tenants) flows across departments as well as up and down the management hierarchy. Because it does not suffer delays or distortion from passing through departmental 'silos', the information is timely and accurate, which means that management decisions are well-informed and effective.

Assessments of the other companies indicated that most had a predominantly Structuralist organisation, where rules and procedures governed how the organisation worked, but in a bureaucratic way that leads to 'silos'. This hinders the sharing of ideas and knowledge across the organisation and the adoption of new ways of working.

Company A had a level 3 process capability, moving towards level 4. Level 3 is 'defined process'. Level 4 is 'Managed process'. That means that the organisation was in control of its systems and processes. They had been able to introduce some standardisation across the organisation and staff were achieving a good level of efficiency.

The other companies had a mix of level 1 (ad hoc process) and level 2 (repeatable process) – each group were doing things in their own way, with a distinct lack of compliance to any standardised processes.

The contrast was significant:

- Company A had a very strong customer and social focus – helping their tenants is why they come to work. This was less evident in other companies, although this varied, with some of the smaller companies showing a closer relationship to their communities.

- We did not find any evidence of silo working or tribal tensions in Company A, but the others all had tensions and distrust between members of the team which were disrupting efficiency and information flow.

- Operational managers in Company A knew that their staff would come to them for help, so left them to deal with day-to-day problems. This left them time to concentrate on planning ahead and dealing with non-routine issues that needed their expertise. The same could not be said about the other companies. In one case the level of distrust was high enough to cause concern whether they could function at all.

- Most of Company A's processes were computerised and standardised across the organisation. The best of the other companies had introduced some computerised systems, but we noted instances of staff working around the system to achieve results and no attempt was being made to improve the system.

- Staff in Company A were fully consulted if changes were needed – in fact most of the improvements in the past year had been suggested by the staff, who were then encouraged to put their ideas into practice. We did not see any evidence that this was happening elsewhere. In two of the companies a strong command and control culture meant that people were told when changes were planned but they had no real input to the change process.

- Trust was high in Company A and information flowed across the organisation as well as up and down, with no distortion or delay. Everyone had direct access to the CEO if there was something they wanted to discuss or alert him to.

- The silo culture in the other companies meant that groups tended to keep information to themselves and only communicated upwards by means of formal reports. The CEOs were visible in all of the companies but none operated a similar open-door policy.

- The CEO in Company A had brought in consultants to harness good practice from other industries to help him develop a sharing culture. Some of the other companies had used outside consultants but only to set up IT systems and re-engineer processes.

Conclusion: the CEO was right to worry about the difficulty he was going to face in developing meaningful collaborative relationships with the other companies. In particular, any attempt to bring in shared services, using standardised processes, would founder on their lack of capability. Any collaborative projects would run the risk of being unrealistic in terms of benefits, timescales and the level of resource allocated to implementation.

Outcome: A staff secondment programme was agreed, whereby a number of managers and staff from Company A were placed into the other companies and their counterparts brought into Company A for a 3-month period. A number of cross-company task forces were devised to develop and implement solutions to specific problems faced by all 8 associations. Finally, a series of efficiency workshops were set up to analyse processes and propose a common set of systems, for implementation (budgets permitting) in the following year.

Index